VUKANI MAKHOSIKAZI

South African Women Speak

VUKANI MAKHOSIKAZI

South African Women Speak

Jane Barrett
Aneene Dawber
Barbara Klugman
Ingrid Obery
Jennifer Shindler
Joanne Yawitch

First published in June 1985 by:
Catholic Institute for International Relations
22 Coleman Fields
London N1 7AF

c   CIIR
    Vukani Makhosikazi Collective

Edited by Ingrid Obery

Design and Artwork by Ingrid Obery

Cover by Caroline Cullinan

Typesetting by Setbold

Printed by Sigma Press

ISBN 0 946848 807

Distributed in South Africa by:
Order of Preachers
P.O. Box 815
1560 Springs

UK trade distribution by:
Third World Publications
151 Stratford Road
Birmingham B11 1RD
England

ACKNOWLEDGEMENTS

Throughout the process of writing we drew unabashedly on other people's experience and expertise. We asked various individuals to carry out interviews, to translate interviews, to give us information, take photographs and to comment on drafts. We would like to thank the following people for their contributions and support.

Reading drafts: Jackie Cock, CIIR London, Cedric de Beer, Isobel Hofmeyr, Gilbert Marcus, Rita Ndzanga, Leila Patel, Lisa Seftel, Jenny Schreiner, Zina Mnguni

Interviews: Aninka Claasens, Pauline Stanford.

Information: Black Sash, Linda Chisholm, Rob Collins, Joyce Dube, Liz Floyd, Hannchen Koornhof, Amanda Kwadi, Norman Manoim, Albert Nolan, Kathy Satchwell, David Webster.

PREFACE

Vukani Makhosikazi was written by a group of Johannesburg women who have participated in a women's study group since 1979. We are:
Jane Barrett: General Secretary of the Transport and General Workers Union.
Aneene Dawber: Speech and hearing therapist and part-time worker with Christian women's groups.
Barbara Klugman: Researcher at the Health Information Centre.
Ingrid Obery: Editor at South African Research Services.
Jennifer Shindler: Researcher at the South African Institute of Race Relations.
Joanne Yawitch: Rural field worker at the Black Sash.

In 1982 the Catholic Institute of International Relations asked us to write a short booklet on women in South Africa as part of a series. As white intellectuals with university training we felt the booklet was a good opportunity to share with our fellow South Africans, some of the substantial research we had done on women in South Africa. The challenge was then to rewrite academic work in an interesting way, accessible to others who were also concerned with change in South African society and women's position in it.

Through our work and broader involvement we recognised the need to document the experience of women in South Africa. Also, that it was necessary to understand their oppression as Africans, as members of the working class and as women. We agreed to focus the book on African women since this would reflect the experience of the women most abused by the process of apartheid and capitalism, the women who are at the centre of the struggle for meaningful change.

Although we locate the position of women within a class framework, in the book we draw out those factors which comprise their specific burden. These include the assumption of differing sexual roles in the family and male dominance in sexual relationships. As a result women shoulder responsibility for the household and children. Women are also drawn into the labour market at the lowest levels of employment — capital conveniently assumes that they are supplementary earners within the family.

Women's position in society raises specific organisational problems. Domestic work is the main form of employment for African women. Domestic work and housework isolate women from each other, locking them into a daily experience of solitary suffering. These women have little chance to move out of these narrow confines and identify with other women. It is all the more difficult for them to identify with men. As domestic workers women may be completely separated from their men. As wives they may be dominated and maltreated in their own homes.

Women often lack confidence especially in the company of men. They accept that men are the 'actors' and 'thinkers' in society. But above all, women are isolated by lack of time. They must cook, clean, look after children and look after husbands.

These are some of the problems which must be addressed successfully in order to include women in political struggle. It follows then that women are most likely to rally around issues like child-care, health and the spiralling cost of living which makes it so very difficult, if not impossible, to feed, house and educate their children.

In unions, youth and community organisations the trend has been to avoid issues fundamental to women's oppression. Women's sexual oppression has created a divide between men and women. During interviews women often said, 'Men are useless somebodies.'

The challenge is to recognise this division as a common problem and work out a way to ensure the involvement of women and men as equal participants in the struggle. This is not to say that men can decide what moves women should make. A male activist said, 'Men won't change the problems that face women, that's a fact of life. Until women deal with them they will continue.'

For these reasons we stress the importance of developing women's organisation. Just as a trade union addresses workplace problems, a housing committee problems of rent, so a women's organisation can address problems which face women as workers, wives or mothers. These organisations can also give women the political experience they do not get elsewhere. Women's organisations should then help to clarify how these problems can be confronted in other forms of democratic organisation.

Shortly after we started this project Ingrid went to Europe. She returned to find that our planned booklet on women had evolved into a once-edited mountain of paper. Ingrid agreed to edit the book and rejoin the group for the process of completing it. She reworked that draft and gave the rest of us the energy to complete it.

Much of the material in this book has been drawn from research done either as individuals or as a group. We met regularly to discuss work done and to plan the framework. This was a slow and difficult process — but also a very exciting and meaningful one. We have also drawn heavily on our organisational experience with women. This book reflects our opinion as a group rather than that of any specific mass-based organisation.

Interviews and quotes in the book that are not referenced come either from research done for the book itself or from research done for one of the following works:

Barrett, J : Knitmore: 'A study of the relationship between race, class and gender', B.A. Honours Dissertation, University of Witwatersrand, 1981.

Cock, J , Emden, E , Klugman, B : 'Child-care and the working mother; A Sociological investigation of a sample of urban African women.'

Klugman, B : 'The Political Economy of Population Control in South Africa', B.A. Honours Dissertation, University of the Witwatersrand, 1980.

Shindler, J : 'The effects of recession, influx control and labour-saving appliances on Domestic Service in South Africa', B.A. Honours Dissertation, University of the Witwatersrand, 1980.

Yawitch, J : 'Black Women in South Africa: Employment and Reproduction', B.A. Honours Dissertation, University of the Witwatersrand, February 1980.

Yawitch, J : 'The Relation between African Female Employment and Influx Control in South Africa, 1950-1983', M.A. Thesis, University of the Witwatersrand, 1984.

The intention is not to give a comprehensive account of the experience of women, or of the many forms of organisation and resistance. Rather, we have tried to bring out the main issues as women experience them. So references to individuals and organisations have been chosen by way of example and not to give any particular importance or priority to them. This is specifically so since we are all based in Johannesburg. We hope, however, that the information contained in the book will serve as a useful resource.

The process of writing the book allowed us the chance to speak to a wide range of women about their lives and women have been only too pleased to tell their stories. Most of their names have been changed for reasons of privacy. We would like to thank these women for sharing their experiences with us. We hope that the book gives an accurate reflection of their lives and goes some way towards enlightening other South Africans about their problems and their potential as a force within the struggle for real change in South Africa.

CONTENTS

Introduction   1

CHAPTER 1   5
STAMPED AND DATED LIVES
- Stamped And Dated Lives   7
- Only Locals   13

CHAPTER 2   17
WOMEN AT WORK
- Women's Labour, Cheap Labour   19
- Labour In The Suburbs   27
- Johanna Masilela — Let Me Make History Please   39
- Working for Knitmore   45
- While The City Sleeps   53

CHAPTER 3   57
LAST IN THE JOB QUEUE
- Farm Work For Life   59
- Working On A Factory Farm   65
- Anna Mazibuko — There You Are Under The Cows   69
- Only A Few Chickens   77
- And How Will We Survive?   83
- No Jobs At All   87

CHAPTER 4   95
UNION WOMEN
- Lydia Kompe — Trade Unionist Not Tea Girl   97
- Show The Bosses We Are Equal   111
- Frances Baard — A Mother Will Hold The Knife On The Sharp End   119

CONTENTS CONTD.

CHAPTER 5 — 125
DAY BY DAY
From Crossroads To Khayelitsha	126
Sophie Sigoro — I Get My Pay It's Gone	133
My Husband He Just Looks!	135
Please Sir Can I Have A Baby	141
If You Don't Pay They Will Knock In The Night	149
Liz Abrahams — Release Lies With Us Working People	153
This House Is So Small	157
Maureen Khumalo — No Husbands Or Children Allowed	161
The Colours Of Apartheid	165
Whoever Thought Of This Family Planning	169

CHAPTER 6 — 177
BARREN DRY PLACES
Kammaskraal — They Are Dying Here	179
We Will Not Move!	181
Umgwali Likhaya — Mgwali Is A Home	187
Eva Mokoena — Magopa Is Our Forefathers' Place	189
Dan Mogale — Donkey Work	193
The Men Are Gone	195
Overcoming Despair	197
Growing Good Vegetables At Overdyk	201
We Must Build A Good Car	205
Grace Ledwaba — Growing Tall	207
Tshidi Kompe — We Use Candles To Read	209

CHAPTER 7 — 213
HOLD HANDS TOGETHER
Then The HP Is A Little Bit Less	215
They Came To Pray, To Help	219

CHAPTER 8 — 225
VUKANI MAKHOSIKAZI — WAKE UP WOMEN
She Named Him 'Freedom'	227
Albertina Sisulu — Strydom You Have Struck A Rock	233
The Women's Charter	238
Our Yardstick Is Democracy	247
Taking A Full Bus	253
Prison Cells	259
Until All Women Are Involved	263

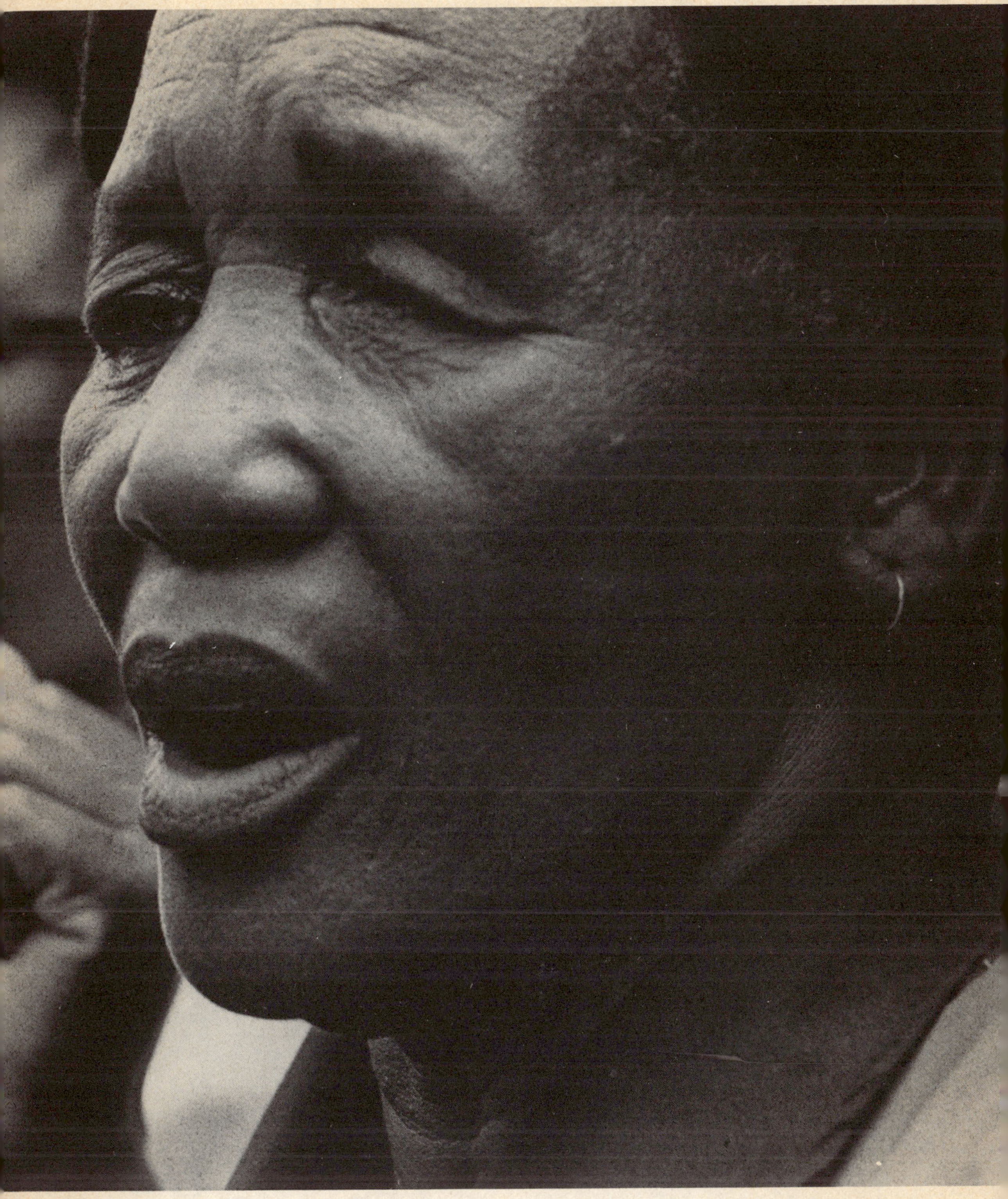

PLACES WE VISIT...

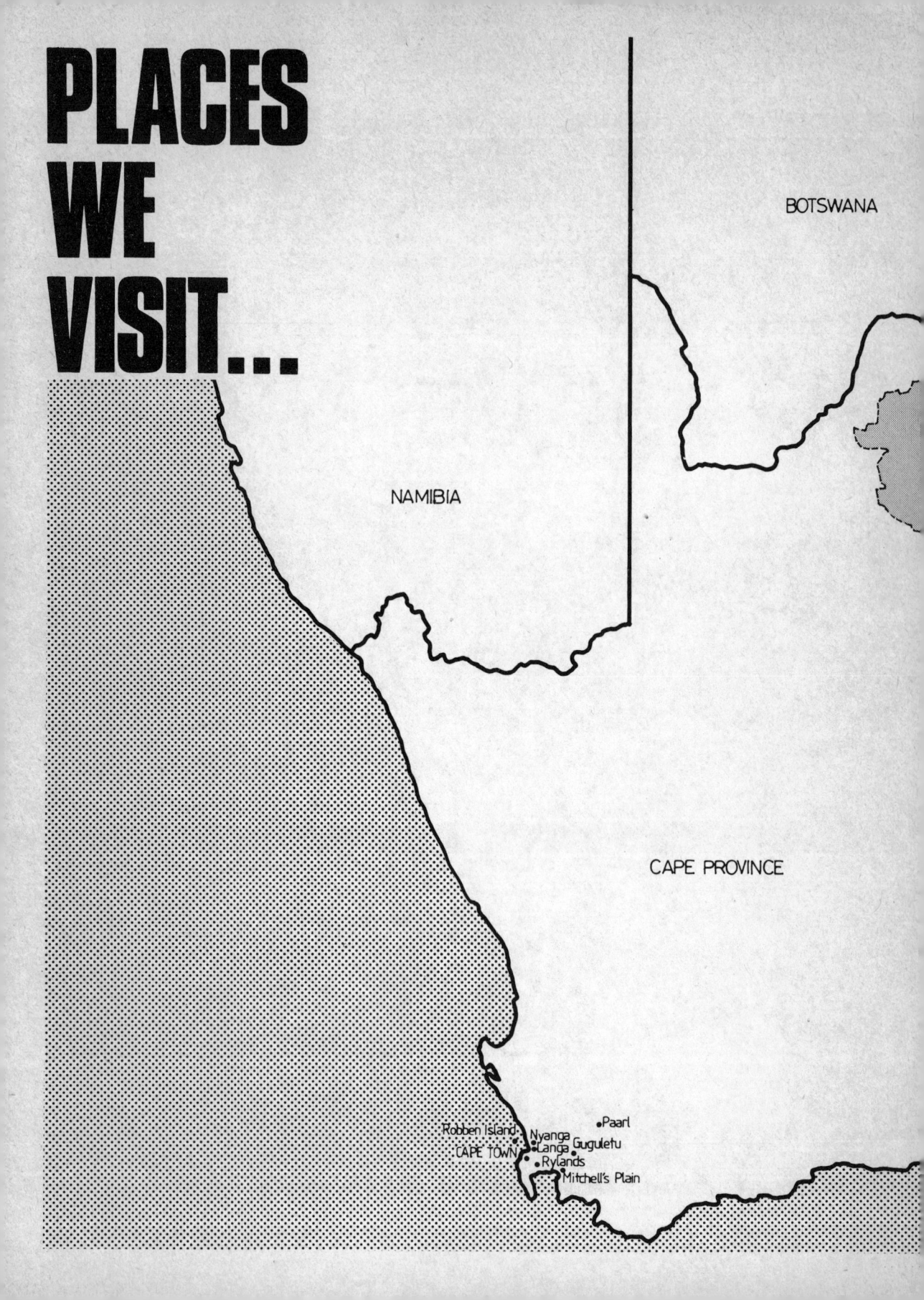

BOTSWANA

NAMIBIA

CAPE PROVINCE

Robben Island
Nyanga
CAPE TOWN
Langa • Guguletu
• Rylands
• Paarl
Mitchell's Plain

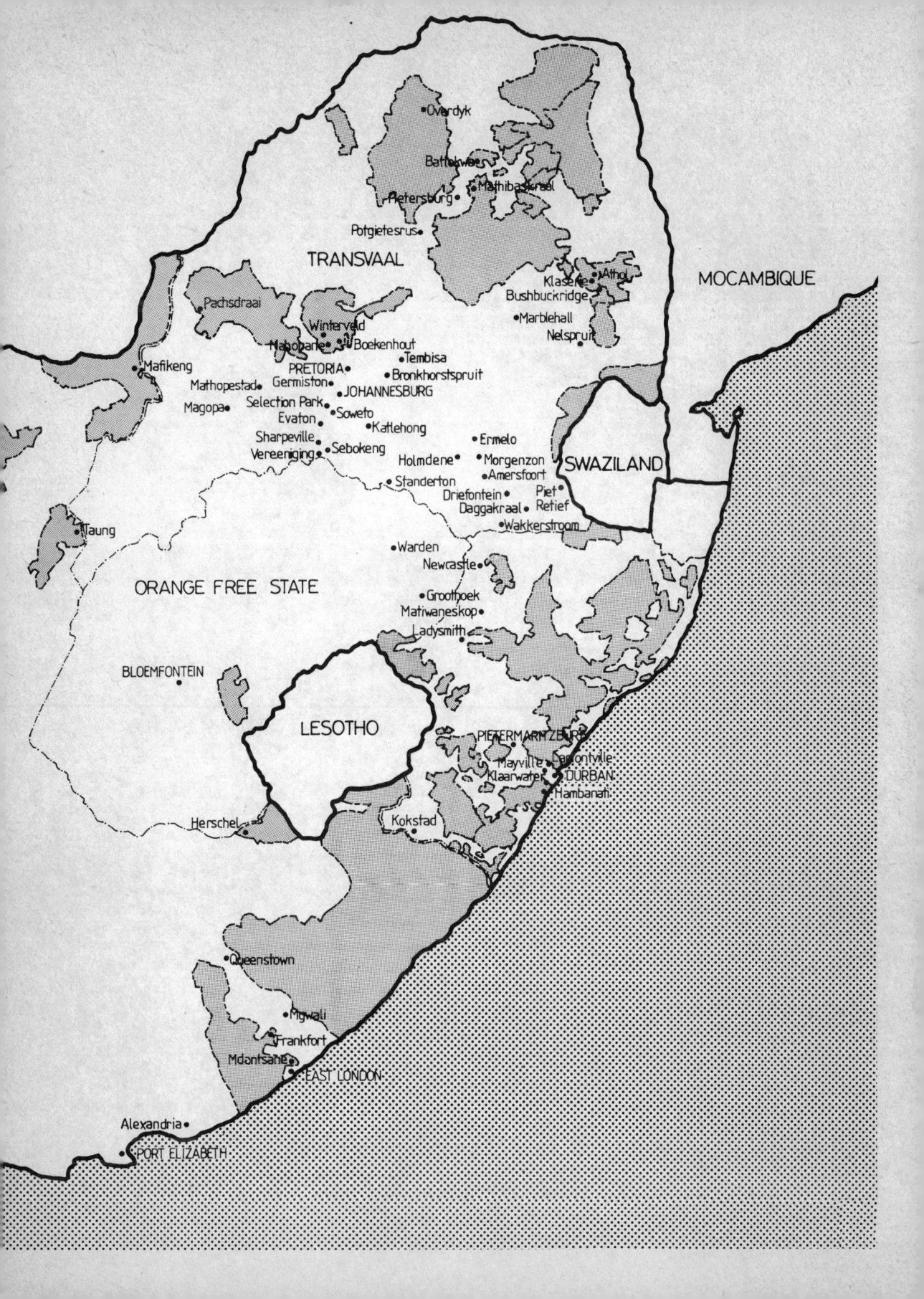

TRANSVAAL
MOCAMBIQUE
SWAZILAND
ORANGE FREE STATE
LESOTHO
Overdyk
Batlokwa
Mathibaskraal
Pietersburg
Potgietersrus
Klaserie
Athol
Bushbuckridge
Marblehall
Nelspruit
Pachsdraai
Winterveld
Mabopane
Boekenhout
Mafikeng
PRETORIA
Tembisa
Bronkhorstspruit
Mathopestad
Germiston
JOHANNESBURG
Magopa
Selection Park
Soweto
Evaton
Katlehong
Sharpeville
Sebokeng
Vereeniging
Ermelo
Holmdene
Morgenzon
Amersfoort
Standerton
Driefontein
Piet Retief
Daggakraal
Wakkerstroom
Taung
Warden
Newcastle
Groothoek
Matiwaneskop
Ladysmith
BLOEMFONTEIN
PIETERMARITZBURG
Mayville
Lamontville
Klaarwater
DURBAN
Hambanati
Herschel
Kokstad
Queenstown
Mgwali
Frankfort
Mdantsane
EAST LONDON
Alexandria
PORT ELIZABETH

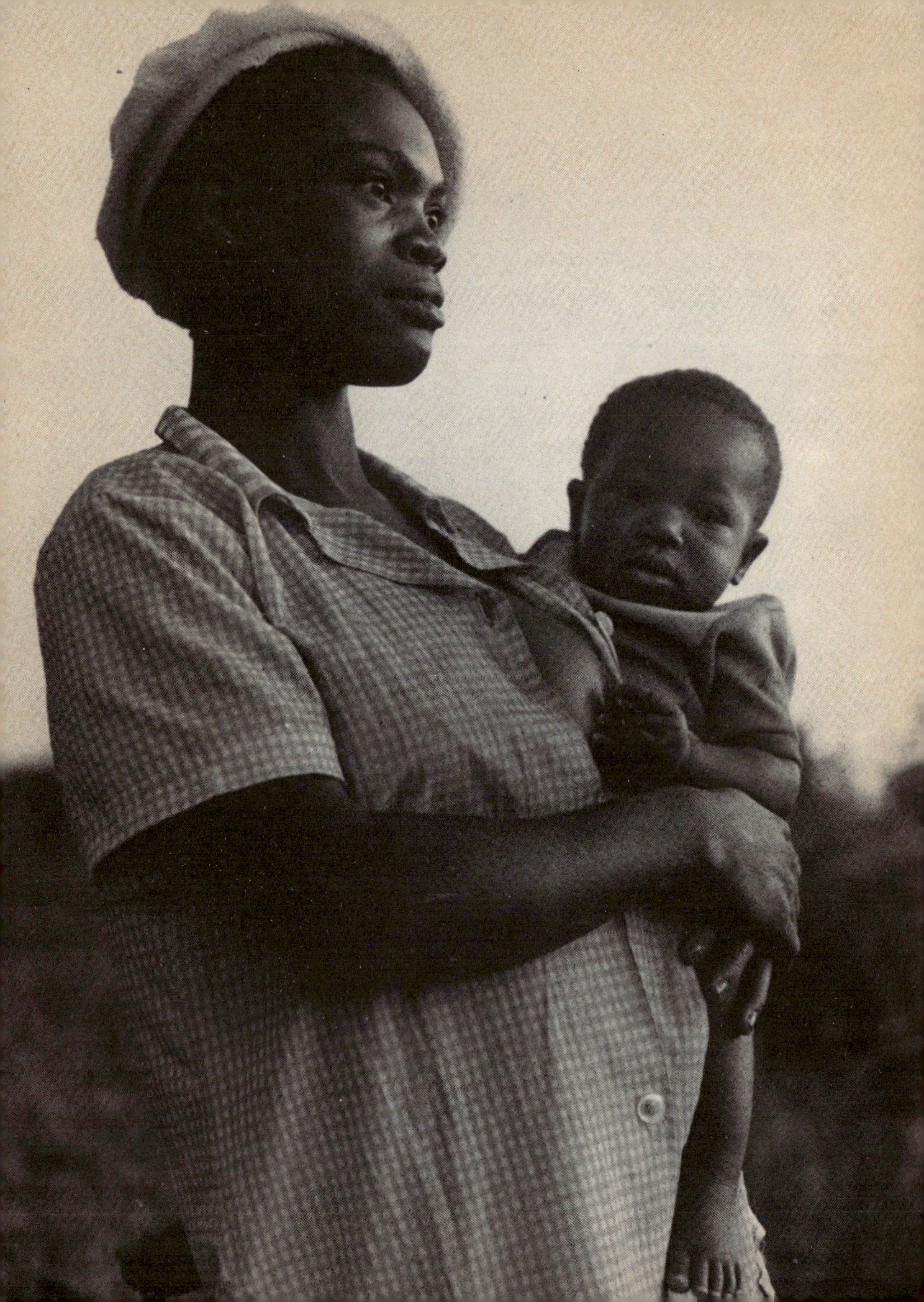

INTRODUCTION

On 9 August 1984, African, white, coloured and Indian women took to the streets of Johannesburg. They held placards saying, 'Women unite against Botha's new deals', and 'Our sons won't defend apartheid', 'You have struck a rock, you have touched the women', and 'GST is killing us'.

The women were saying — these are our problems. They are caused by apartheid and the system of racial and economic exploitation in South Africa.

Why do these problems exist in South Africa and where did they come from? In this book we try to give some answers. In their own words, African women talk about their lives. They speak of their families, their jobs, their joys and hardships.

1984 was not a good year for most South Africans. The economic recession continued. This meant increased hardship for many. Jobs became scarcer by the day. Food prices soared. Local authorities pushed up rents and did nothing to improve conditions in the townships.

And this is just part of everyday life in 'sunny South Africa'. President Botha's 'new deal' — the tricameral parliament — has been set in motion. Based on an entirely new constitution, the parliament has three separate houses. The House of Assem-

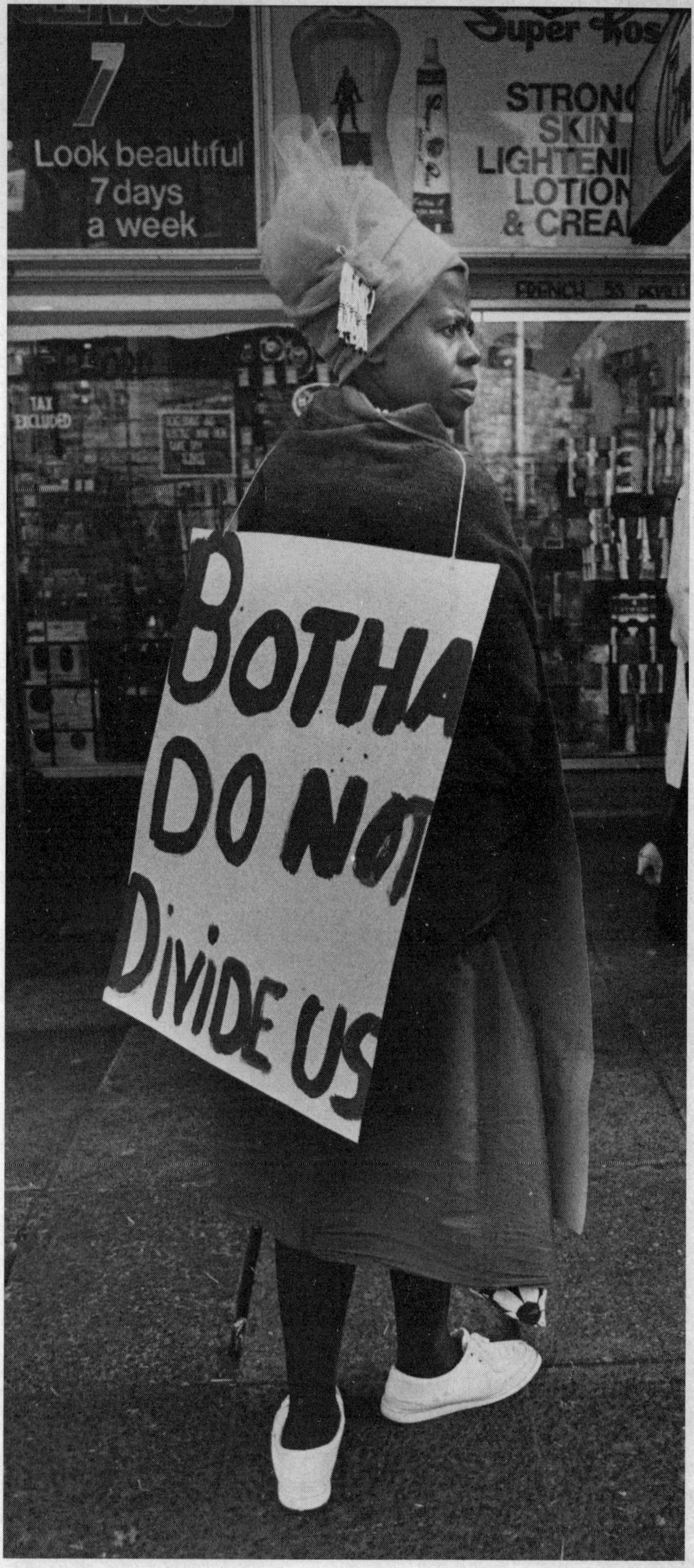
7
Look beautiful
7 days
a week
BOTHA
DO NOT
DIVIDE US

bly for whites, the House of Representatives for coloureds and the House of Delegates for Indians. No house for the Africans.

Elections for the two new houses were held in August 1984. But the elections were marked by low polls, and police violence and opposition protest were more in evidence than eager voters.

There are hints that a fourth house for Africans may be considered in the future — that is those Africans who cannot presently be expelled to the bantustans.

But the new parliament has meant no change for most South Africans. It offers no real power. Terms are still dictated by the white minority, and the State President has powers of veto on all issues debated in all three houses.

The sustained militancy of many communities in South Africa indicates that government solutions will not be easily found.

African school students boycotted school for most of 1984, and there were more students on boycott than there were in 1976. There were community and township protests over increased rents, general sales tax hikes, inadequate township services. Community Councils and the new Black Local Authorities were rejected by most people.

The latter half of 1984 saw townships on the Reef erupting in protest — Tembisa, Sebokeng, Sharpeville, Katlehong, Soweto.

Over 160 people died during unrest in 1984, and hundreds more were injured. Combined student and community demands reflected the growing politicisation of the African population. Even as the recession deepened and workers were retrenched in their thousands, students and workers in the Transvaal called a stay-away in November 1984. It was 80% successful on the Reef.

But the cost of living still spirals, and conditions do not change. The crushing burden of poverty rests on the working class. Most of all it rests on the backs of working class women - especially African women.

This book is about these African women. It does not cover all the issues nor does it answer all the questions. But it does reflect something of the lives, something of the desperation, something of the grit and determination which characterises women in South Africa today.

'Vukani Makhosikazi' explores day to day life in South Africa. What do women working in factories or on farms think? What are their issues and questions and desires? Do these women want to be organised, what do they think of 'politics'? How do they cope with poverty, and sexual and racial oppression? And most importantly what are the problems in organising African women?

Chapter 1

STAMPED AND DATED LIVES

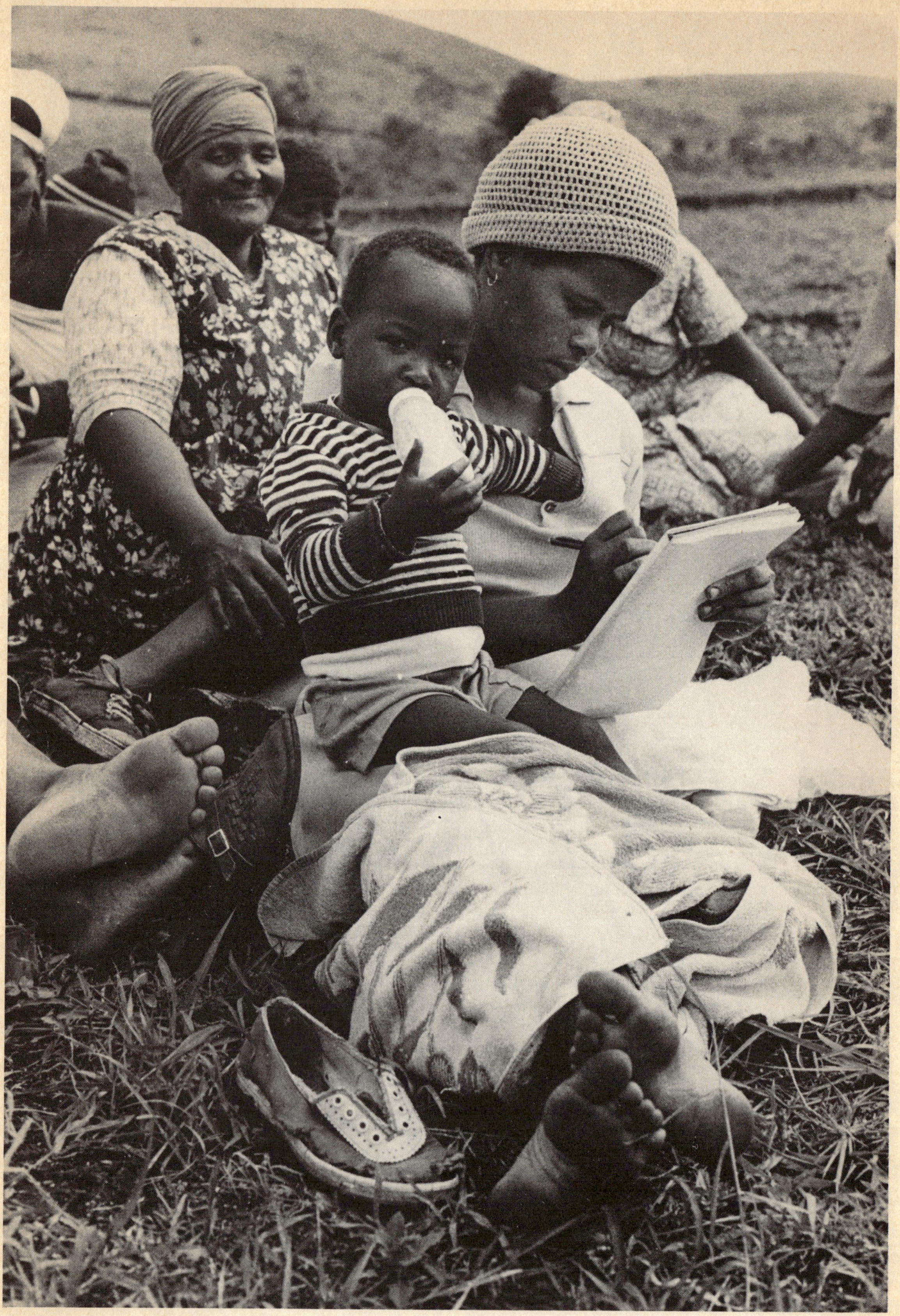

Stamped And Dated Lives

Tryphina Lesea sat quietly in the Black Sash Advice Office. She folded her hands in her lap. She told her story calmly. But her story reflects the desperation which many South Africans feel because of the pass laws.

Tryphina Lesea was born in 1930 in the township near Frankfort in the Orange Free State. In 1946 she came to Johannesburg to live in Alexandra township. Later she moved to Soweto. She worked as a domestic servant in the 1950s and was employed by two people.

The first time Tryphina ever applied for a pass was in 1964. At the time she was selling beer in the township. Once she was sentenced to a six month jail term for selling beer illegally. After that she worked as a char, doing odd jobs for a range of white housewives in the suburbs of Johannesburg.

Tryphina has three children. She married in 1977 but her husband deserted her in 1982.

Although she has lived a relatively peaceful life in the city, Tryphina is in serious trouble. For neither her residence, nor her employment, have ever been reflected in the reference book (pass book) which she took out in 1964.

Because of this, officials will not believe that she is an urban resident who should have the right to live and work in Johannesburg. If arrested for a pass offence, she would probably be deported to Frankfort where she was born. She has not returned to Frankfort since 1946.

Tryphina Lesea has survived in the city for many years. It is possible that even without proper documents she may continue to do so.

But the controls over urban Africans get tighter all the time. Life without documents becomes more and more difficult.

To legalise her status, Tryphina must collect affidavits to show how long she has been in the urban areas, where she has been living and for whom she has worked. With great perseverence she may yet succeed. If she does she will be one of the lucky ones.

For many people the bureaucratic nightmare never ends — the necessity to be documented, stamped and dated, the humiliation, the indignity and the confusing and contradictory orders and demands made by officials. All this means that many people never succeed.

Tryphina has managed to stay in Johannesburg, making a living for herself and her children. Her sisters in the rural areas of South Africa are less fortunate. Over the years they have been stripped of the right to come to the cities to look for work or to live with their families and husbands in the urban townships.

Sara Sibisi's story is a common one. 'I was born in 1946 at a place near Klaserie in the Northern Transvaal. Until I was 13 years old we worked and lived on a white farm. The life there was hard, but even so we had our own plot to plough, and we had some cows and some sheep.

'Then we were chased off the farm. The farmer just told us to go — he gave us no reason at all. What could we do? We just went.

'We trekked to this village and got a plot. They promised us land but it never came. Our troubles really started here. My youngest brother got sick. He swelled up and died. He was only a baby. It was hunger. It was very painful. Then my other sister.

'My father was working on the mines at that time. But there was little money. As soon as I could I decided to go and work and help my family with food and the other necessaries.

'So in 1963 I went to Jo'burg and found a job. I was very lucky at that time. It was before the passes were so heavy.

'I went on contract and worked in Southdale. Then the people left. They went to Durban. It was in 1970. I went to stay with my aunt in Soweto.

'I had piece-jobs for some time. Then I had my firstborn. I went home at that time. Since then I have never found a job. Not a proper job.

'When I ask at the commissioner they say only farm work.

Controls over urban Africans get tighter all the time. Life without documents becomes more and more difficult.

City jobs are only available from a commissioner's office. The work on the farms it is heavy, and the money is little. It can kill people.

'I tried to go back to Soweto without a contract and work. But it is harder than ever before. Many madams are scared now. They say they'll get caught if they have a "girl" without a pass. I tried at the pass office. But they just say I must go home. There is no work for "girls" from the homelands.

'I was arrested too. That was bad. So I came home. Maybe I will work on the farms. But only for a while. It's bad.'

Since the 1950s all African people in South Africa have had to carry passes. Since then there have been increasingly strict

Amanda Kwadi of the Federation of Transvaal Women, protesting on the streets of Johannesburg on 9 August 1984, National Women's Day.

Paul Weinberg

measures to control the rights of African women to live and work in urban areas.

Tryphina Lesea's story reflects the problems of those women who were already in urban areas before the extension of passes to women in 1952. Because her life was never properly and officially documented, she now has serious problems.

Sara Sibisi on the other hand, has problems that stem from the way the system is implemented. Soon after women got passes, far fewer women from the rural areas were allowed to move to towns to work. Women could move to town if their husbands had permanent urban rights. Then they could get Section 10 (1) (c) rights as well.[1]

In 1964 even this loophole was closed and an administrative embargo was imposed on the entry of women into urban areas. Sara, in 1964, was one of the last lucky few to be able to work legally in town.

This embargo was only fundamentally challenged in 1980 when a migrant worker, Mr V Komani won his case against the Western Cape Administration Board. He had applied to the Supreme Court for an order allowing his wife to join him in Cape Town on the grounds that because he had urban rights, she should be able to join him.

The government was quick to act on this newfound loophole. In August 1982 a new amendment was passed to the Urban Areas Act. It stated that a man could only bring his wife and children from the rural areas if he had a house of his own in the urban area. The critical housing shortage makes this impossible for most male workers, and especially for poor people.

And so rural women remain, excluded by law from any chance to find work in urban areas, or from living with their husbands.

Influx control and the pass laws are one of the fundamental pillars of apartheid. The severity with which they are implemented is not likely to lessen. Despite much talk of reform of the influx control system, it has only got progressively worse.

FOOTNOTE:
(1) In terms of section 10 (1) of the Black (Urban Areas) Consolidation Act of 1945, no African would be allowed to remain in a prescribed area for more than 72 hours unless that person:
a) was born in the area and lived there continuously;
b) has worked continuously in the area for one employer for ten years, or lived continuously in the area for not less than 15 years;
c) is the wife, unmarried daughter or son under the age of 18 years, of any person who qualifies to be in the area in terms of section 10 (1) (a) or (b), and provided that he/she has entered the area lawfully and lives with his/her husband or parents;
d) has been given permission to remain in the area by a labour bureau official. Before giving this permission, the official must take into consideration the availability of accommodation in the African residential area.

Only Locals

There is a total embargo on African women from the rural areas entering the urban areas. Many women choose to ignore it and come to town because they are desperate for work.

But it is not easy for them to survive. They must work illegally because it is impossible for them to get legal registration. This means that they live in fear of arrest and employers can pay extra low wages for more work.

Because they are illegal they cannot challenge low wages or bad working conditions and can be dismissed easily.

Until 1979 it was quite easy for women to work illegally as domestic workers. But since the introduction of the R500 fine for employers with illegal workers, employers are reluctant to take the risk.

Influx control bureaucracy is effective. In August 1984 Sipho Sibisi asked a white friend at work to help a young friend of his. His friend, called Gladys Mbazima, comes from Daggaskraal, an area in the Eastern Transvaal. Daggaskraal is presently under threat of removal.

Gladys has been unemployed for six years. There is very little labour recruitment from her area, and especially no women recruits. So she came to Johannesburg to look for work,

Pass Laws

and because she wanted to live in the city for a while.

Gladys found a room to live in Alexandra township north of Johannesburg. But because she was not registered for work, she was in the township illegally. Without the proper stamp in her reference book she could be fined or imprisoned if arrested (currently about R30 or 30 days).

Sipho asked his friend to register Gladys as a domestic worker. This formality would allow her to move more freely in Johannesburg — without the constant fear of arrest. She would continue to live in Alexandra, but could always say she was sim-

A street in Alexandra township

ply visiting there.

Gladys's problem was not easily solved. The official behind the desk at the Albert Street Pass Office took one look at Gladys' reference book and said, 'We can't register this "girl". She's from the homelands. You must go to Polly Street labour bureau and find a local "girl". There are hundreds of them there to choose from. We can only register locals'.

The official said that there was nothing particular about Daggaskraal. Any woman without permanent residence in the urban area of the Witwatersrand cannot register for employment.

Pass Law Arrests and Prosecutions[1]

A total of 206 022 people were arrested by administration board officials and the South African Police for pass-law offences in South Africa in 1982, which was a 28,3% increase over the 1981 figure of 160 000. The 1982 total amounted to the arrest of 564 people a day, or 23 per hour, or one person every 2,5 minutes. Mrs Helen Suzman (PFP) said that the figures showed that urban Africans had not been affected by the climate of reform as far as the pass laws were concerned.

Arrests in the major metropolitan areas: (official figures)

	SAP		Administration boards	
	1981	1982	1981	1982
Bloemfontein	957	856	3 055	5 885
Cape Peninsula	250	145	13 444	15 867
Durban	1 879	7 169	1 089	688
East London	503	2 151	49	64
East Rand	5 060	9 873	23 878	35 891
Johannesburg	36 582	40 223	3 994	6 886
Pietermaritzburg	4	—	—	—
Port Elizabeth	5	76	749	2 648
Pretoria	13 248	19 499	6 192	64
Soweto	24	1	—	—
West Rand	2 590	2 573	9 504	10 549
Total	61 102	82 566	61 954	78 542

FOOTNOTE:
(1) Survey of Race Relations in South Africa 1983, p262,263.

Chapter 2

WOMEN AT WORK

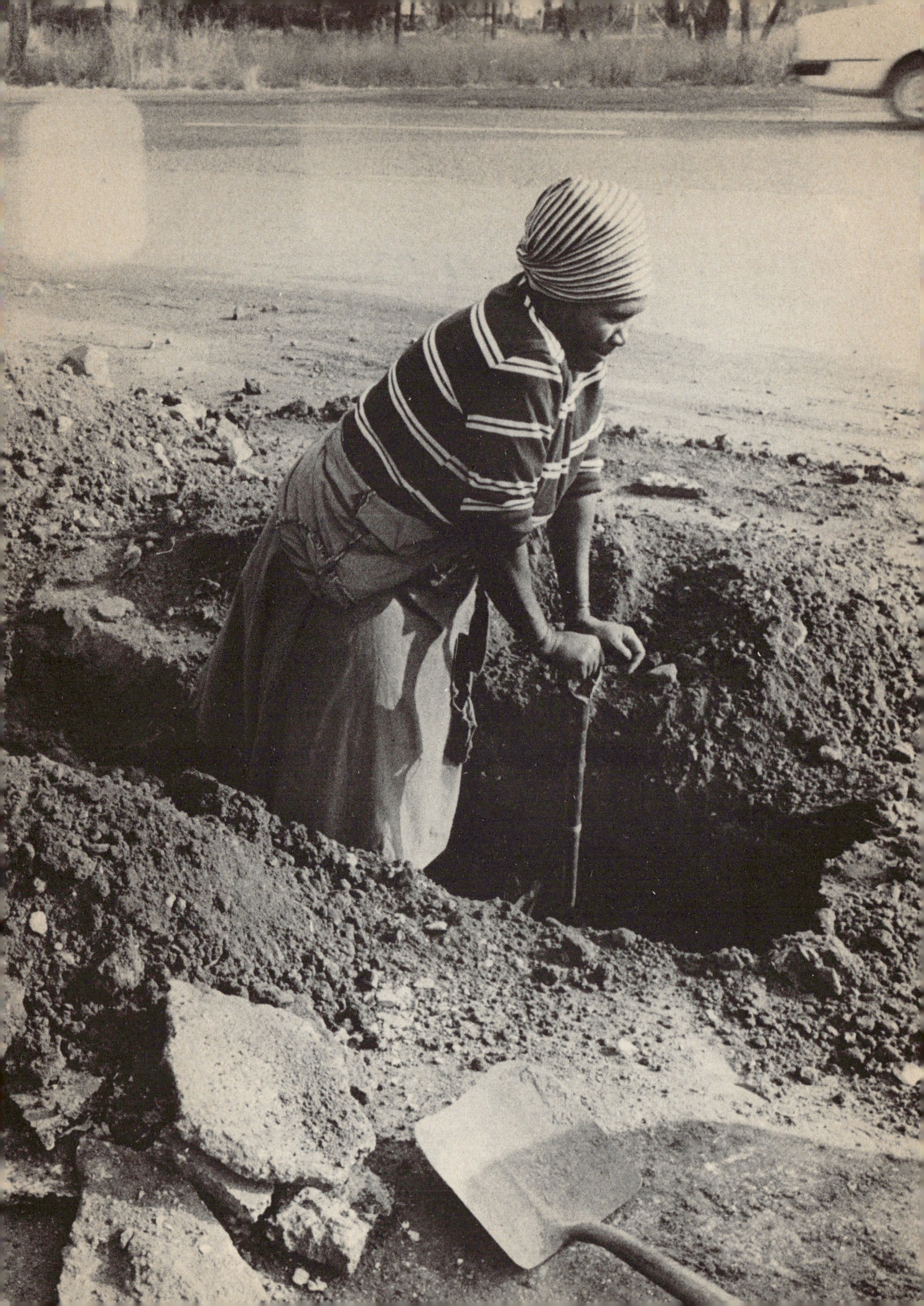

Women's Labour - Cheap Labour

In the 1980 census, three-quarters of all African women were recorded as not having a paid job. Most of them worked at home. Their work in maintaining households and bringing up children is of course as vital to the economy as any other task. But it is not paid, and the lack of income is a desperate problem for many South African women.

For those who can find a paid job, conditions are very poor. The work is strenuous and hours are long. They are paid low wages, and the day's work continues when they get home. Unemployment is very high, and women in the urban areas are desperate for work. Women who become pregnant may well lose their jobs because many others can take over.

The type of work women do is changing. In the last century women were employed only as domestic servants or on farms. But since the beginning of this century, many more African women have moved to urban areas. At first most worked as domestic workers, but since the 1950s women are increasingly being drawn into the industrial economy. They are employed in factories, in commerce and other services.

Women at Work

Percentage of employed African women per sector:-

	1981
Agriculture	16.6%
Mining	0.4%
Manufacturing	10.7%
Electricity	0.1%
Construction	0.6%
Commerce	15.0%
Transport	0.6%
Financing	1.3%
Services	54.4%
Total Number	1 754 000

Because they are unskilled and because their position in urban areas is insecure, African women are paid low wages.

There are specific reasons for the way African women have been drawn into the labour force. Because they are unskilled and because their position in the urban areas is insecure, African women are paid low wages. The history of the clothing industry in South Africa is a good example of how this has happened.

The Clothing Industry — then and now

Before the 1920s clothes were made mainly by individual tailors. They made garments from start to finish, and often owned their own sewing machines. Most tailors were white men.

The demand for bought clothes grew. Many business owners saw that they could make huge profits by mass producing cheap clothes. So they set up factories and eventually the private tailors were squeezed out of business.

Work was done on production lines in the factories. Large numbers of white women were employed. They were paid very low wages. Many of them were young Afrikaner women whose parents could not support them in the rural farm areas.

In 1938, 60% of workers in the clothing industry were white - most of them women. Coloured and African workers (male and female) were only employed as labourers, while the white women were the sewing machinists and cutters.

As time went on many of the young white women started to find clerical jobs which were better paid. By 1953 only 28% of the workforce in the clothing industry was white.

This was a time of great growth in the industry. From 1947 to 1957 the output grew by 738%. But the number of workers only increased by 151%. This was because employers brought in more and more machines.

Machine operators' jobs became less complicated. Each worker did one tiny job on her machine and then passed the garment on to the next worker. So it was also taking less and less time to make a garment.

But employers were finding it difficult to find enough white workers to fill the jobs. When they started to employ African workers the white workers were afraid that they would also be replaced.

And so in 1957 the first job reservation legislation was introduced in South Africa. A government investigation recommended that blacks should be employed in the industry, but that certain jobs should be reserved for white workers. These jobs were the more skilled jobs such as machinist and cutter. Only whites could be supervisors.

Employers did not always keep to the restrictions, but white people could be sure of a job. But employers continued to employ Africans because of the shortage of white workers who were prepared to accept the working conditions in the clothing industry.

For a short time employers employed African men rather than African women. Until 1954, because they were defined as 'pass-bearing natives', African men were not covered by the provisions of the Industrial Conciliation Act. So they could be paid wages which were lower than the wages negotiated by the Garment Workers Union in terms of the provisions of the Act.

African women were not defined as 'pass-bearing natives', and so they were covered by the Act and received any negotiated wages. The Garment Workers Union won this right in 1948.

After 1954 all Africans were defined as 'pass-bearing natives' and employers began to employ African women at the lowest rates. From 1960 to 1980 African women were employed in greater and greater numbers as these figures for the Transvaal clothing industry show:

Employment in the Transvaal clothing industry - 1960-1980

Race and sex	1960	1970	1980
White male	212	200	124
White female	3 745	1 104	362
Coloured male	395	493	334
Coloured female	6 185	6 134	2 437
African male	3 636	3 116	2 054
African female	4 207	13 859	15 368
Totals	18 380	24 906	20 679

From this history we can see that the race and sex of workers in an industry often changes with changes in the way goods are produced (the change from tailors to factories); shortages of certain groups of workers (the shortage of white women workers in the 1950s); and the wages employers can pay certain groups of workers.

So it is wrong to say that African women are now employed

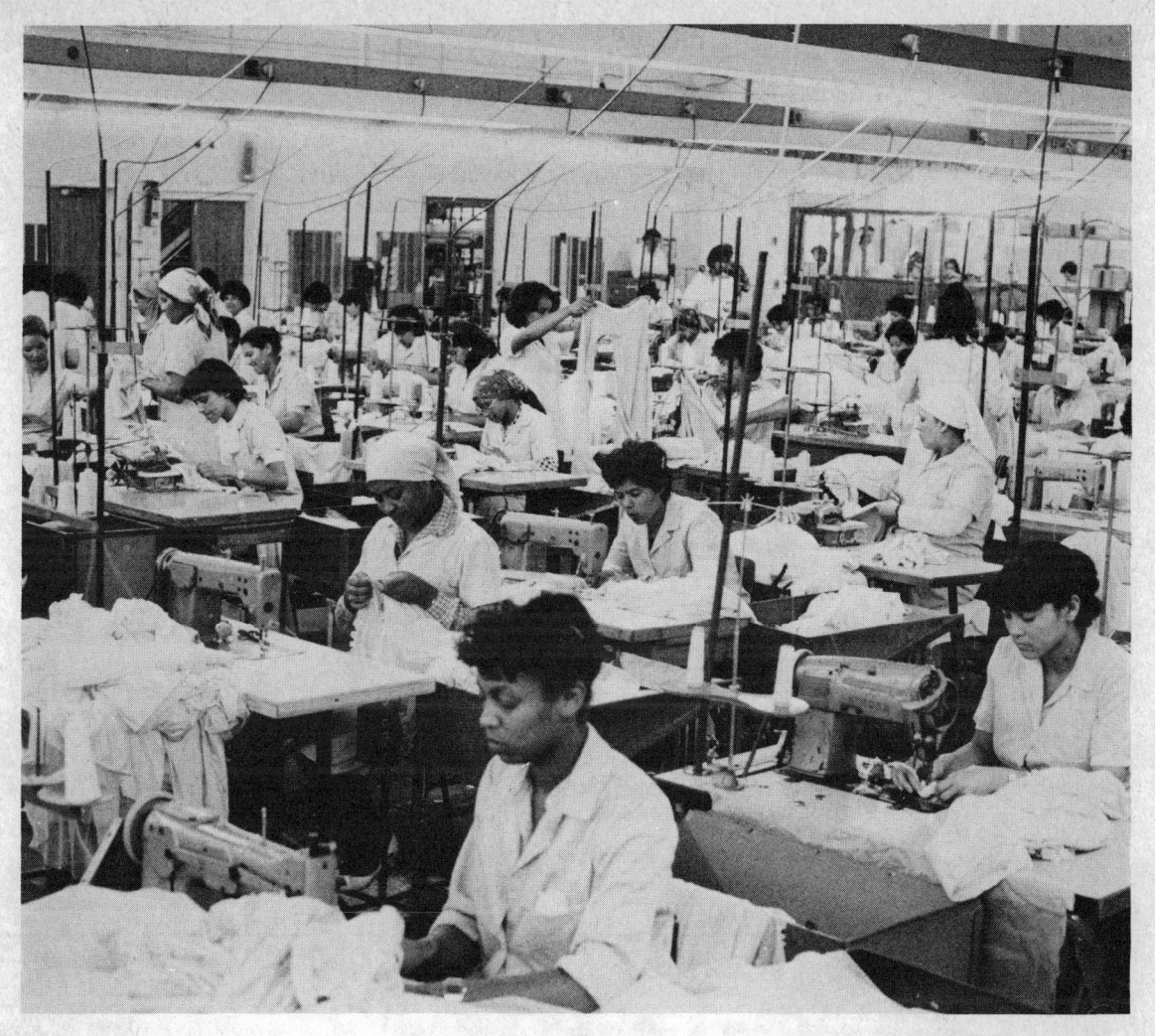

A garment factory in Cape Town.
'The race and sex of workers in an industry often changes with changes in the way goods are produced.'

in certain industries just because they are women. Even so, many people still think this.

For example, Mr Thomas, general secretary of the Clothing Industrial Council in 1981 said, 'I think that by natural upbringing women are more geared to operating sewing machines and making clothes and so on — you know, in your home division women are considered to be the ones to make clothes etc and this is the natural outcome of things. And so women have tended to go into garment manufacturing.' He forgets that male tailors used to make clothes to sell only 60 years ago.

But today, the clothing industry nationally employs more coloured than African women. This is because most of the industry is in the Western Cape. African workers have, until very recently, been excluded from working in the Western Cape by the Coloured Labour Preference Policy.

Other industries show a similar pattern to the garment industry. For example in the textile industry, new machinery and technology were introduced in the 1960s. Unskilled workers

Women at Work

were needed, and by bringing in African women, many jobs could be downgraded and undervalued. By 1981, almost half of all textile workers nationally were women.

The food industry is also dominated by women workers. African women are also starting to replace men in the shoe manufacturing and furniture manufacturing industries.

Sometimes employers bring in women workers in an attempt to undermine the organised strength of unionised male work-

Jimi Matthews

ers. But this does not mean that women workers are less militant than male workers in South Africa.

More than half of employed African women work in services. These are jobs like office and shop cleaning, laundry work, cooking, domestic work and municipal services. Many African women now work as clerical and sales staff in the commercial sector.

The general pattern has been that African women find a

foothold in jobs out of which coloured and white women have moved, and for which African men are considered less suitable or more expensive. African women for instance make up 43% of the female workforce in manufacturing.

Urban African women can find jobs — even if they are badly paid with terrible working conditions. But rural women cannot even get to the towns to look for a job. The pass laws and influx control keep these women in the bantustan areas.

In these areas and just outside of them there are some places where a tiny minority of women can find employment. Part of government policy for many years has been to encourage business to invest in the bantustans.

Border Industries

During the 1960s only 11 500 jobs were created by 'border' industry schemes. From 1970 to 1978 only 34 000 jobs were decentralised to border industries.

In 1981 the government started a massive new incentive for decentralisation. Companies would be compensated for the longer-term disadvantages (eg railage rebates) and would also be helped with short-term finance problems (eg cash subsidies on the wage bill, interest subsidies, reimbursement of relocation costs). In fact, wage subsidies in the Ciskei often exceed the total wage bill. These wage subsidies in the Ciskei can last for seven years.

Investors did respond. In 1981 private sector capital investment in projects in 'decentralised' areas was R245 million. In 1982/3 R2460 million was invested, and in the latter part of 1983, the figure was R3324 million.[1]

The incentives have attracted foreign companies too. The United Kingdom, Taiwan, and the United States are the largest investors in these areas.

There were 1593 projects proposed during 1982 and 1983. About 40% of these have been implemented. These projects represent 116 036 jobs.

FOOTNOTE:
(1) South African Labour Bulletin: Vol 10 No 3, P118.

In the following pages we look more closely at African women at work.

Labour In The Suburbs

On a sunny Sunday afternoon in a white South African suburb many African women sit on the pavements. They sit in groups, or alone, talking and resting, making the most of the few hours they have for themselves. These women are domestic workers.

Most of them are migrant workers from the rural areas. They have little or no formal education. They usually have nowhere to stay when they come to the towns. So live-in domestic work is their only option.

Why domestic work?

Evelyn Molefe was born and brought up in Mafikeng in the Western Transvaal. Her father raised cattle and her mother worked around the house. She left school in the middle of standard four, the sixth year of schooling. Her parents could not afford to send all the children to school, and her father did not believe that girls needed education.

'Well what could I do with so little education and I had to

earn some money because my family were so poor. All I could do was domestic work to earn some money.'

Flora Monamodi's parents died when she was a baby and she went to live with her grandmother in Taung in the Northern Cape. When she finished standard two, she left school.

'I wanted to become a nurse but you can't do that with so little education. The only thing I could do was housework. I looked for work around Taung but there were no jobs so I came to Johannesburg. I didn't know anyone here so I had nowhere to stay. I walked around every day looking for a job and in the night I slept anywhere. The good thing about this job is that you get somewhere to stay.'

Johanna Mokone was born in Taung. Her father worked on the mines in Kimberley and her mother was a seamstress. Johanna left school in standard six and first worked as a trainee nurse on the mines. But she did not like this work. She then tried sewing and selling clothes but did not make enough money. So she came to Johannesburg to look for a job.

'Well I really had a hard time finding a job. I tried to find work in a factory but there were no jobs there for me. I had to find work in a house where I could also live because my cousin was unable to support me. Anyway I did not have much learning or any skill so I have to do this type of work.'

Because women can live-in at the place of work, domestic service in South Africa, unlike Britain or the United States, has remained a full-time rather than a part-time occupation. But economic recession means that many employers can no longer afford the services of a full-time domestic worker. Employers then do their own housework, or employ someone once a week.

So domestic workers have been forced to find several different jobs for different days of the week (piece-work). Piece-work is a difficult way to earn a living. Full-time work generally pays better than part-time work and offers the additional perks of free board and lodging. It is also difficult for women to find a job for every day of the week.

Families

Most domestic workers have homes and families in the rural areas. Children are generally looked after by a family member, usually a mother or a sister or older child. To support her family the domestic worker must send most of her wages home. Low wages make it very difficult for domestic workers to support their families. Many are single parents. Others are married but their husbands seldom give them money.

Evelyn Molefe has three children in Mafikeng who are being

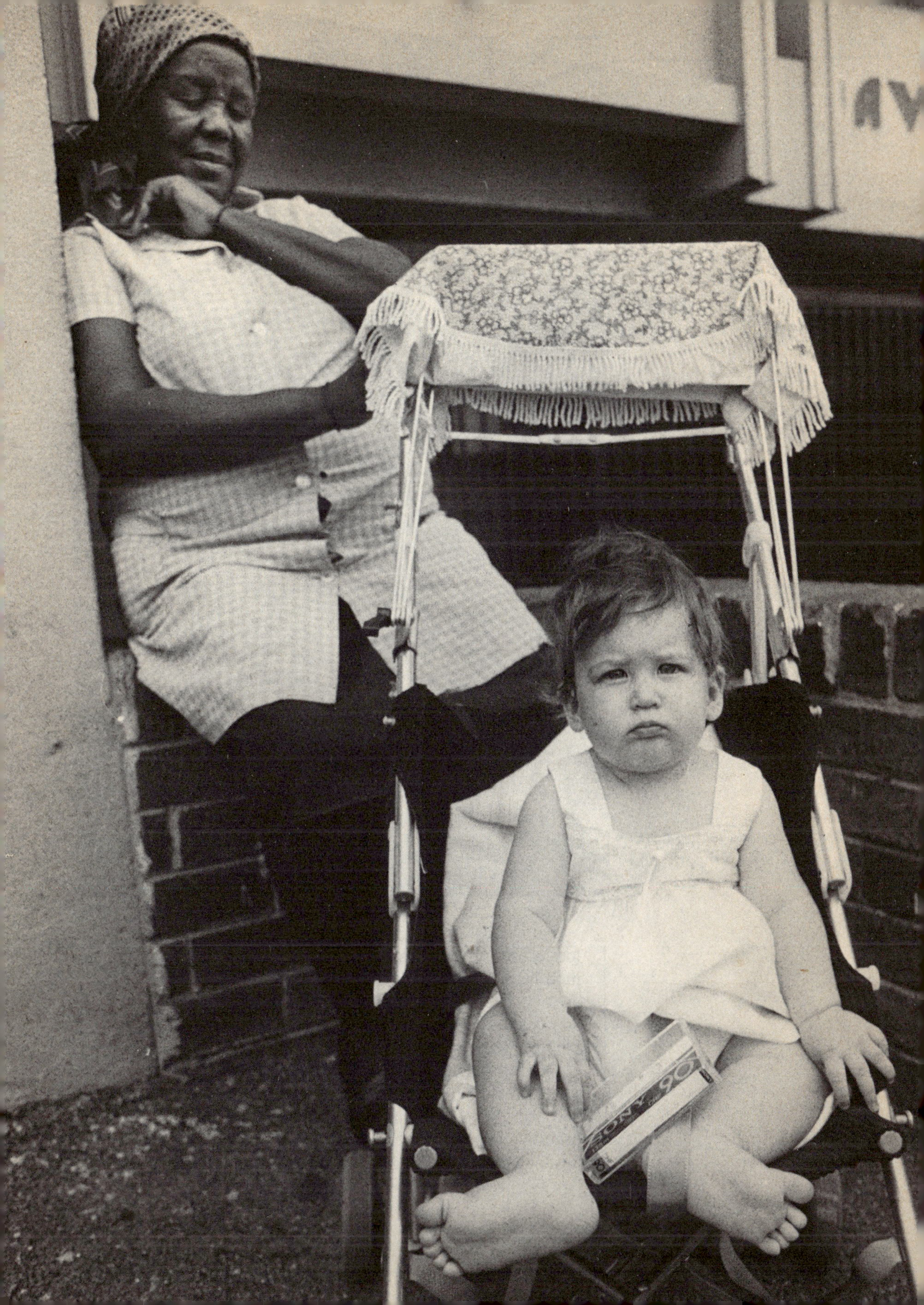
SONY
90

Domestic Work

Domestic work is tedious and tiring. Workers start early and finish late.

Omar Badsha

looked after by her mother and an old uncle. She earns R50 per month and sends most of it home.

'It is a very big struggle for me because I don't have a husband so there is no-one to help me with money and I want my children to finish school and get good jobs.'

Eldah Mthuludi has two children, a son and a daughter. She said, 'I am getting R65 every month. I can't save any money because I send most of it home, and my mother and children can't live on what I send them — they are starving. I have this husband but he is useless. I don't know what he is doing and I don't know what he does with his money but I never see it.'

Sarah Kumalo has four children, including a two-year-old

baby. They all live with her mother and sister and sister's children in Newcastle in Northern Natal. Sarah earns R61 per month. With this she supports her mother, her sister and all the children.

She said, 'For me it is a big struggle every day. My sister doesn't have a husband so she has no money and she is too lazy to work. My husband — he works on the mines — sends some money every four months or so and things are a bit easier. Sometimes I speak to my madam — I say my children have got no clothes, or I must buy new schoolbooks or something. She will give some money, but usually I just don't know what to do.'

Daily life

Domestic work is tedious and tiring. Workers start work early and finish late. If they live-in, they may always be on call. They can be asked to babysit, make tea or run up to the shops even when they are not on duty. The job usually includes cleaning, washing, ironing, cooking as well as looking after children.

Eldah Mthuludi said, 'I work very hard. I must start work at seven o'clock in the morning and I only finish at 8.30pm after they have finished eating supper and I have washed up the dishes. Every Friday I have to work until 10.00pm because my madam had people for supper. On Saturday nights I have to come in and look after the children because the madam and master go out. I don't get paid any extra money for doing it.'

Rebecca Sepule starts work at 6.45am. She sets the table and cooks breakfast for the family. While they are eating, she eats her own breakfast. After washing up the dishes she cleans the house. This includes making the beds, vacuuming all the carpets, dusting, washing the kitchen and bathroom floors and in winter cleaning the fireplace.

Rebecca finishes cleaning at about 11.00am. Then she starts on tasks which are done only once a week, washing the windows, cleaning the stove and the fridge, polishing the silver and brassware or cleaning the walls.

Rebecca makes lunch for the children when they come home from school. After washing the dishes and eating her own lunch she does washing and ironing. At about 4.00pm supper must be started. After supper she washes up the supper dishes and knocks-off at about 7.00pm. If her employer has visitors in the evening she comes in at about 9.00pm. to make tea.

'This job, it just makes me too tired. I'm on my feet all the time and you can't just stop and do nothing and rest your feet. The madam might think that you are too lazy and she might tell you to go.'

Flora Manyono works from 7.00am until 7.30pm. She described her job, 'You can never get away. You can never have a bit of time for yourself. I can be eating my lunch and my madam will decide she wants something from the shops or a cup of tea. I must jump up and go then — I can't even finish eating. If she calls and I'm doing something I must still go. I can be cooking or ironing and the child will cry — and she'll shout "Flora, Cindy's crying". She's just lying on her bed or talking on the phone or her friends are visiting. I'm working and she's doing nothing but I must always be there.'

Time off

Unlike factory work, domestic work has no laws which set out hours of work, leave, or terms of contract. These arrangements are usually laid down by the employer. A domestic worker's hours and time off depend on her employer's life style. Time off, which includes time off during the day to eat, days off during the week and annual leave is usually arranged so that the employer is not inconvenienced.

Evelyn Molefe starts work at 7.00am and finishes at about 6.00pm after the family she works for finishes supper. She does not get much time off during the day.

'I stop to drink a cup of tea in the morning for five minutes. I don't eat any breakfast. After I finish cleaning at 1.00pm I cook my food and eat lunch. I must be back inside the house at 1.30pm to wash the lunch dishes. I eat supper after I knock off.'

Agnes Ceba has Thursday afternoons off and on Sundays she can go off after she has washed the breakfast dishes. On Thursdays she does some shopping for herself and then sits in the park with her friends. On Sunday she attends church. She gets two weeks paid leave in December when her employers go on holiday.

Betty Nene is in her sixties. She suffers from high blood pressure. Fortunately she has a fairly lenient employer. Betty usually takes an hour off for breakfast and two hours for lunch. She has a full free day every Thursday and every second weekend she goes home to visit her family. At the end of the year she has one month's paid holiday when her employer either goes on holiday or employs a temporary domestic worker.

Eldah Mthuludi said, 'I don't get any time off for breakfast. I sort of eat while I work. I don't get any time off for lunch either so I don't eat anything. How can I eat anything when I don't get time to cook it?'

Eldah's days off are Thursdays for the whole day and Sundays after lunch, as well as one week-end off a month. On

Omar Badsha

A domestic worker and her employer in Grey Street, Durban.

Thursdays she attends literacy classes and on Sundays she goes to church. She gets three weeks paid leave a year in December and her employer employs a temporary domestic.

Low wages, little security.

There is no minimum wage level for domestic workers in law, and the wages paid are extremely low.

Eldah Mthuludi said, 'I am earning R80 per month now which I think is alright, but you can always do with more money. When I started here 11 years ago I got R18 per month.'

Agnes Ceba said, 'I am earning R50 per month now. When I started here in 1975 I got R30 a month but things are still hard. I've got children you know, who are with my mother. I have to send money home every month — whatever I can afford — and it doesn't leave much for me. Still I get better money than my friend so I can't really complain.'

Flora Manyono said, 'I'm now getting R70 which is too little. How can I look after myself and my children on this money? You work very hard in this job and earn very little. My madam, she does nothing, but she can live in this nice house and have fat children. My children are hungry.'

Many employers justify the appallingly low wages paid to domestic workers by arguing that the accommodation and food provided is the wage. Any real cash paid is simply pocket money. They forget, of course, that if domestic workers live-in they are on call virtually 24 hours a day. They also forget that their employees have families to support. The food provided is usually leftovers or inferior meat and porridge.

In the sample of domestic workers interviewed in Johannesburg some felt that they would never lose their jobs unless they chose to leave. Others felt they could be fired at any time.

Eldah Mthuludi said, 'If you complain, you can lose your job. She'll tell you about all the other people who come to the door looking for work.'

And Betty Nene said, 'I don't think that my madam will ever fire me because I do my job well.'

Some domestic workers felt that it would be easy to find another job if they were dismissed or if they left their present job. Others felt that it would be difficult.

Betty Nene said, 'I've got a pass [reference book] so it should be easy to find another job. But others aren't so lucky.'

Johanna Mokone 'It won't be easy to find another job because there is a lot of unemployment. I don't know what I'd do if I couldn't find a job.'

Eldah Mthuludi said, 'It will be a big struggle to get another job. I had a friend who couldn't find a job for five months. She had to come and sleep with me here.'

Lizzy Nkosi and Emily Moloi were both fired from their jobs as domestic workers. Their stories show how vulnerable women domestic workers are.

Lizzy Nkosi said, 'From 1981 I found work for seven months in Linden [a Johannesburg suburb] at a flat. Unfortunately my son passed away and whilst I was arranging a funeral plan to bury my son, my madam shouted and wanted to know as to how long do blacks take to bury their dead.

'She further said I was continually ill. She paid me R33 a month. Every time I went to the clinic the madam would subtract 50c or R1 from my wage. She did not allocate money for transport. It was the real exploitation that I suffered that made me not keen on begging for the job.'

Emily Moloi, 'I have worked at Mr Core's house as a general worker. Starting at 6.00am and knocking off at 7.30pm depending on how early I have finished my housework. Later on I would go in to wash all the dishes after they had had supper. I was earning a sum of R60 a month. On weekends I was starting at 6.00am to 1.00pm. It was a sleep-in job.

'When my madam went overseas I was left to look after her

Bee Berman

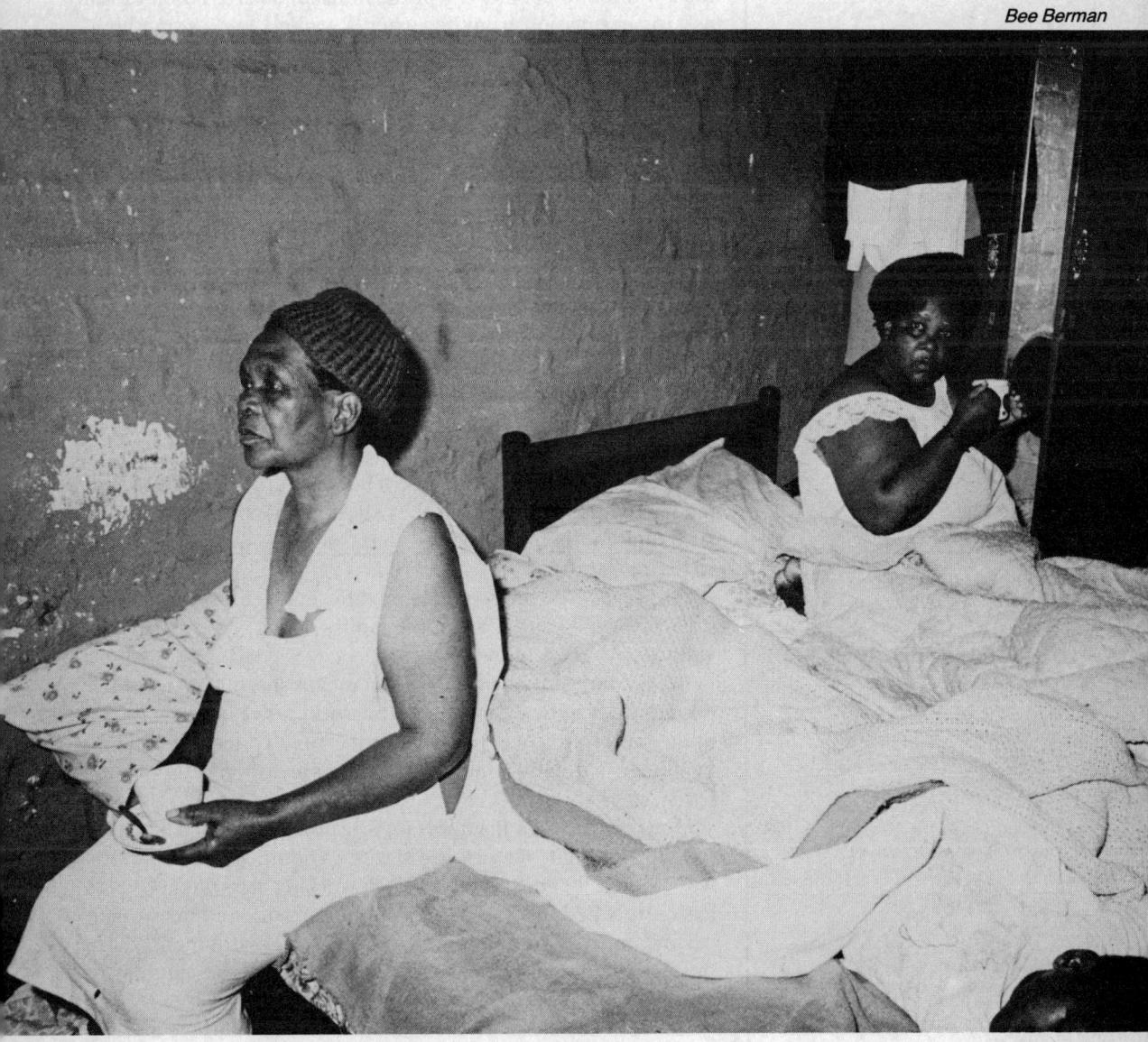

4.45 am: Mrs Bam and Miriam, domestic workers, with children and grandchildren still sleeping, get up to be at work at 7.30 am.

mother who was old. One day when the granny was out shopping I started cleaning the house. When I was scrubbing the floor I couldn't find where the scrubbing cloth was. I used an old towel which was used for the dogs.

'When she came back she asked where the towel had gone to. I told her that I had torn it into pieces. She swore at me and told me I wanted to act like the prime minister's wife. I didn't even ask for permission from her when I wanted to do something. She said, do I think I am a madam and she is a black woman? I could see I could not work with her co-operatively. So there was no point in resisting to leave.'

Being 'part of the family'

Very few domestic workers enjoy their work. They see their employment as a fact of life, an inescapable necessity. The following comments are typical.

Johanna Mokone said, 'There is nothing good about this work, but at least I have a job.'

Agnes Ceba, 'I hate being called "the girl". I am 48 years old now and I'm still a girl.'

And as Rebecca Sepule says, 'The children are terrible. I am older than their mother but they shout at me and swear at me. And their mother says nothing. They would not say those things to their mother.'

Employers see the relationship differently. Employers often say, 'She's a "gem". Part of the family in fact. And she's marvellous with the children.'

Being 'part of the family' seldom means sharing in any of the household facilities. Most domestic workers live in single rooms in the back-yards of employers' properties. Toilet and washing facilities are usually minimal. The rooms are often without electricity and heating.

Housework plays an important role in society. But it has traditionally been given a very low status. In South Africa, domestic work is usually performed by black working class women. This has entrenched the low status of both the work and the women performing it. White children grow up in an environment where the African domestic worker is the servant and the parents are the masters.

Rebecca Sepule said, 'My madam works in an office and she is too tired to clean the house when she comes home.'

Flora Manyono said, 'She has lots of friends and she plays tennis and cards. She has no time to do housework.'

Sarah Kumalo, 'She's lazy.'

Betty Nene, 'Oh no she's a lady, she couldn't do this type of work.'

Some employers said that they employed a domestic worker because they worked. Many more said that by employing a domestic worker, they were able to devote more time to their children. However most of them were quite shocked at such a question. In a country where her mother and grandmother before her and all the people around her employed domestic workers, most white South African women have never questioned their reasons for employing domestic workers. They have assumed this as a right.

Collective organisation

Domestic workers are isolated from each other. So collective negotiation and action is almost impossible. It is difficult for domestic workers to act together and demand higher wages and better working conditions in the way that factory workers can.

A number of organisations have been set up throughout the country to deal with domestic workers' problems. They include the Domestic Workers and Employers Project (DWEP — Johannesburg), the South African Domestic Workers Association (SADWA - Johannesburg), and the Domestic Workers Association (DWA — Cape Town). DWEP tries to 'make better maids' by upgrading the skills of domestic workers in order to make them more valuable, whereas SADWA and DWA have tried to model themselves on trade unions.

All the organisations have asked for minimum wages. Some have demanded the establishment of standard contracts of employment. But they face major organisational obstacles: in the isolation of one worker from another and in the complete lack of legal protection.

Lesley Lawson

Johanna Masilela, 'I enjoyed looking after children.'

Johanna Masilela

Let Me Make History Please[1]

Johanna Masilela was born in 1916 in the Vereeniging district where her father was a sharecropper.

'They called it Hokieslagt.....it was a farm. It was Willem Petoor's, an Afrikaner. My mother and father were working on the farm. He used to get many bags of mielies. They shared the products they grew. The farm was the boer's [farmer] farm, but he gave us land too — we'd share.'

As a child Johanna 'helped' at the farmer's house. Her father was a sharecropper. So he had to let the farmer use his family as workers. Johanna worked in the 'boer' house until she was eight years old and sent to school. When she was very young she became disabled.

'When I got crippled my mother was out working clearing the crops. That day I was left with my aunt and my mother's grandmother. We used to have fowls, pigs and oxen. We had a lot of pigs. Big pigs! My aunt "abbad" me - tied me to her back - but then she got on top of the pig like a horse. Then when the pig said "Hrruggh" I fell. I was small, about three years.

'When my mother came back, she found me crying, but they

didn't tell her what happened, frightened perhaps that she might hit my aunt. So the foot swelled up slowly until at last they told her. You know in those days doctors were not too experienced. In any case it shrank. But I could not walk because I walk on my toes all the time.'

In time Johanna learned to walk well enough to make the long walk to school each day.

'It was a long distance from the place where we lived to where we attended school. Yes, so I used to walk with my crippled foot. And sometimes my father used to take me by horse cart and fetch me when it was raining or when it was very cold.'

Johanna was the eldest of four children, two brothers and a sister. After she had been at school for a few years her family moved to Evaton outside Vereeniging where, until the 1950s freehold title was available to Africans.

'My father bought two stands when he felt we were working hard and were staying too far from school. My mother told him it was no good any more. She could no longer work. At the farms you work hard, yes. They were getting old then so we moved. We went to Evaton, nearer the school we attended.'

In 1927 Johanna was very ill and could not attend school. 'I got very sick. My neck and legs were full of sores. I couldn't walk. And then I went to hospital at Driefontein. They called it Thembisa Hospital at that time. I went there in November 1927 and I was there until March 1928.'

Johanna only attended school until the age of sixteen. After passing standard six she left school and stayed at home helping her mother.

In 1932 she left Evaton and went to live with her uncle in Sophiatown. She worked as a domestic servant in Mayfair, a suburb of Johannesburg.

'That's all I could do, because I only passed my standard six. I could work because I was brought up working. So there was nothing that could defeat me. You could only tell me to do this, do this, do this, and I used to do it.

'And funnily, I never got nice easy jobs. I used to get hard-working jobs. Scrub the floor, polish everything, washing, ironing, cooking, you know everything. But I could manage to do that, even with my foot. And if I got a job and wanted to leave, they didn't want me to go because they knew I was hard working.

'In 1937 I got a job at Melrose working for Mrs Sinclair. And there I got a very nice job because I was a baby-minder. That child was Shelley. I used to care for her. Sometimes her mother used to just leave and go to Durban and leave me with the child and the granny. Because she knew I knew everything about the child.

'That child used to be like my child. Because she never used to bother me. If the child was sick I phoned the doctor and the doctor came, treated the child and I nursed the child until she was well.

'It's where I got that experience of caring for children. I knew in the morning what I must do for the child. And I got to know if you are with a child you must know how to talk to a child, make speeches for her to laugh, read books and so forth. Everything, bath her, wipe the napkin clean. Must be clean, yes.

'Cook for the child. Until she could feed herself a little bit and while she eats I'm also eating, making speeches for her to laugh, so that when she laughs she eats more than when she's just quiet.

'Sometimes I had to go and take a blanket and go and sleep next to her so that she can see me and then she can start sleeping. And when she was asleep I would go out to my room. It was nice, I enjoyed it. It gave me very good experience.

'But Newlands was nearer Sophiatown. I thought, let me work in Newlands to be nearer home, so I can go home every day to see my husband. I used to do a lot of washing too. After giving one madam her washing, I'd go to the other one and wash. The following day I start ironing.'

Johanna's first child was born in 1940, the second in 1944, the third in 1951 and last in 1956.

'When I got pregnant I left the first job. Until I felt all right, then I worked and after that I used to leave the job, get the baby, and after two months, I start working again.

'I put the baby on my back and I used to let her sleep under the table where I was working, perhaps ironing. When she wasn't sleeping, she would go to the kitchen or out into the yard. The child I used to take with me to work was my second boy. The oldest one stayed with my mother in Evaton. I left him with my mother from when he was about six months.

'They didn't mind when I brought my children to work, my Europeans didn't. You know if you're a hard worker she must get soft. Because she knows that what you are doing is freeing her. But if you are lazy then she will notice everything, and she will say, 'You come with your children, you waste my time. You're caring for your child, you don't do my job. The thing that must be very important is the work.

'In 1957 Sophiatown was removed. They moved us to Meadowlands in Soweto. We didn't like it. You know, getting a new place which you're not used to, you think you're going to suffer. Because Sophiatown was near town you could take a bus. That time it was pounds, shillings and pence. Take a tickey [two and a half pence], go to town, tickey back. We thought it was going to be very far if we have to go to the station and travel by train. But then it just happened that we forgot about that

Child Minder

Sophiatown removal.

'But I couldn't work in Johannesburg. It was too far. So I would go and buy fruit in the Indian market and come and sell fruit. In 1959 I got a job doing ironing in Empire Road, Parktown [Johannesburg suburb]. So I used to go once a week and leave that young one with my neighbour. The elder one would come back from school, bring the brother, so I'll find them at home.

'When we came in this house in Dube I had to do something else. A friend of ours was a teacher. They had a baby and he

Lesley Lawson

Child Minder

came to me and asked me where I was working, so I said, "I'm ironing in Empire Road."

'Then he said, "Can't you look after my baby? Just tell me what that madam is paying you for doing her ironing. I will pay you more!" And I thought how can an African like myself say he can pay me money? I talked to my husband and he said, "Ag just try it."

'So I left the ironing and I started caring for that child. Now the gate was open. Every day I got somebody else who wanted me to care for their child.

Johanna, her husband and family members.

'Had it not been for these children, where would I be now? The mothers bring their children in, they fetch the children and take them. It's not for me to travel by train.

'Right now I can't board a train because of my leg. I can't lift it high. I can't even get into these kombies [minibuses]. I can get into a car because a car is flat.

'Now where will I get that work? So I used to enjoy it. They used to help me, because if you're gnarled, your life is no more good. And you still see you're earning something. Can't you say thank God. Those children, they took me as their real mother. Because they don't know their mothers. They used to see their mothers late in the afternoons. I was the mother.

'But since 1983 I'm tired, I'm tired, you know. My leg is getting tired, paining sometimes. The muscles must have a rest. I've worked too hard. I'm crippled. With my leg it just becomes loose, as if I don't feel it. Sometimes it gets cool and sometimes it's hot.

' Since 1981 it started feeling like this. So I think I must give it a rest. I've been standing too long with it and doing hard work. I must say, thank God he has kept me standing with one foot all these years.

'When you are sick, each time a child cries you feel miserable. So I don't want to feel like that. I'm no longer in my same mood. Even if I see a child I could help by doing something, but I have no patience to stand up. When your whole body's tired you become cruel, so it's not nice. A child needs a very good care and you must be broadminded, have a nice feeling.

'All these years I've been so nice and I've enjoyed doing it. Now when I see it's no good I don't want it. I don't want to have children because I see now I haven't got patience any more. But I used to have a nice life, a very nice life.

'So I've left my history somehow. I'm happy that I've got somebody who will introduce me. Let me make history please. Johanna Masilela. My number is 827.'

Working For Knitmore

Only a small proportion of women are employed in manufacturing. It is also the sector where women can best organise themselves and so advance their wages and working conditions. In industry women work in groups, they are not isolated from each other as in domestic service on farms or in services.

Women workers are concentrated in particular industries - notably food, textiles and clothes and in lesser numbers in the shoe, electrical machinery, leather, wood, furniture, non-metal minerals, rubber, paper and chemical industries.

Women workers are used in border industries (factories on the borders of bantustans), and in factories inside the bantustans (where in 1976 they were more than half the manufacturing workforce). In the bantustans there are no regulations for minimum wages or working conditions and trade unions are restricted or banned in most. That is one of the reasons why industries are attracted to invest there.

Working for Knitmore

In the clothing and knitting industries, women make up 83% of the workforce. Knitmore is the largest knitwear factory in

A Clothing Factory

Johannesburg. It employs nearly 600 people. Knitmore makes socks and jerseys for some of the major chain stores.

The factory was established in 1927. Originally it gave a form of 'sheltered' employment to the dependents of miners who died of miners pthisis. The first Knitmore workers were mostly white and female. It was only in 1941 that the first black labour (male) was employed. At this time white female unskilled labour was in short supply.

Many women working in industry are permanent urban dwellers, not migrant workers. Often their mothers were domestic workers, and they themselves came to the cities as children.

But like most women, they were unable to get much education and training. Girls tend to be forced to leave school at a younger age than boys. So they can legally take urban jobs

A supervisor checking garments at Knitmore.

— but being unskilled, they must look for unskilled jobs, jobs from which they can easily be fired and replaced if they cause trouble.

The histories of the women of Knitmore reflect this general background of women workers in industry.

Maureen Zakwe was born in Kokstad near the Transkei. She came to Johannesburg as a child in 1947, when her mother came to seek work as a domestic.

Miriam Njoli, who grew up in Queenstown in the Eastern Cape, came to Soweto in 1964 to study commercial courses. She did not have the resources to even begin her studies, and so looked for work in industry. Her first job was as a messenger and she later became a presser in Knitmore. Miriam lives in a hostel.

Maria Rampai who is 21 years old and lives with her parents, left school after completing standard seven to learn dressmaking. After qualifying, she could not find a job so joined Knitmore as a machinist. Her mother also works in the knitting factory as a presser. Her father is a driver for the West Rand Administration Board.

Mary Tsotsi has just started her first job as the age of 19, for R19 a week. She found the job through her sister who is employed in the clothing industry.

Dora Makhathini was born in Ladysmith in Natal and came to Johannesburg as a child. Her mother was a domestic and her father a miner. She has worked for Knitmore for 11 years as a presser.

She said, 'The work is so hot — it is quite a heavy job. But I just get used to it. Where can I get another job, anyway?'

The factory is divided into two sections — one in which fabric is knitted, and one in which garments are sewn together. There are slightly different wages and working conditions in the two sections.

Why are some jobs held by men and some by women? Doreen Ntuli, works with three other African women and one Indian man in the pressing section.

She explained, 'When I started here, there were also men in pressing. But the men were chased away because they said they needed more pay. They were getting more because they were men. The one man on the job is getting more than us because he is a man, and also an Indian. It is not fair, as we are doing the same job.'

Men are generally paid more. In the knitting section, new male machinists started on the same wage as a woman was earning after 10 years' service.

The Basic Conditions of Employment Act of 1983 states that there will be no differences in the mimimum wages of men and women doing the same job. But there is nothing stopping

A Clothing Factory

employers from putting male wages above the minimum. Also, an Industrial Council Agreement, or an in-house (plant-level) agreement can set differing rates for men and women.

The Act does not set out minimum wages for most of the other areas (other than industry) where women work — such as domestic service, farming, or any state employment.

In the pressing section there are more women workers than men. But in the knitting room where machines are kept going for 24 hours, Lena Matambuye was the only woman among 22 machinists.

'There were other women on the machines but they didn't satisfy. I am used to it. It is now like home. But I could never work nightshift because of the children.'

The floor manager of the section explained the lack of women on night-shift differently, 'Men are definitely better operators - partly because of the nightshift. You could never have women on nightshift. I mean sex is a natural thing for everyone, but with these people they don't really mind who they do it with. Even in Germany I think they have legislation against women working at night for the same reason.'

This crude and racist view of the place of women is not uncommon.

Lesley Lawson

The pressure of work

The company insists on hard work and many workers feel overworked. Women from every section voice this.

Maggie Mtimkulu started as a cleaner, but now checks and mends completed jerseys. 'It is a better job — less tiring. But we sit next to each other and we are not allowed to talk. We must just listen because we are stranded. If we talk they are chasing us away. We should work on, rushing all the time.

'That rushing kills us — some jerseys are heavy — when you are turning them all day your shoulders get sore.

'The mending is very difficult. It is a strain. And it's very noisy and dusty in amongst the machines.'

In the next room, six pressers stand over the table-top steam presses the entire day. The floor manager explained how he managed to make them work so hard, 'Last year we were pressing 1 000 pieces a day. I wanted 2 500 pieces and I couldn't get it. One day, suddenly after months of seeing no-one at the door looking for jobs, there were five. So I took them all on. I trained them without firing anyone, but those who didn't pull up their socks I eventually fired. I now have double the production.'

In the sewing section it is the same. Bridget Mokoena, an overlocker, said, 'Here you don't get money, because they just want more and more production, but without caring for you. The wages is my biggest problem. I am a learner in overlocking but I must do the same work as the so-called experienced women. It's the same amount of work but with less pay. They just call us learners so they can pay us less.'

The working conditions are very poor. Maggie Mtimkulu, who complained about noise and dust, contracted TB at 25 after eight years at Knitmore.

The steam presses are called abortion machines because of their effects on pregnant women. The women cutting out the patterns work with very fast band saws. The blades on these saws are completely unprotected.

Wages are low. In 1980 a machinist with ten years' experience earned R45.50 a week, a presser R29 after 11 years, a newly-employed marker just R17.20.

The minimum wages in the clothing industry have been increased since the Knitmore study was conducted. Examples of some of the minimum wages in the Transvaal gazetted in March 1984[1] are:

Transvaal minimum wages - March 1984

Job Description	Min Starting per week	Min Qualified per week	Qualifying Period
Pattern Maker	R 36	R 121.76	4,5 years
Presser by hand	R 36	R 66.30	2,5 years
Sewing machinist (setting sleeves, tailored coats)	R 36	R 79.40	3 years
Sewing machinist	R 36	R 56.00	2 years
Cutter	R 36	R 70.90	2,5 years
General Worker	R 36	R 42.30	1 year

Lesley Lawson

One of the few woman machinists threading her knitting machine — Knitmore.

Minimum wages in the textile industry were last set nationally in December 1975. Some of these wages are as low as R11 a week.

Most women felt 'trapped'. They had no option but to accept low wages and tough working conditions.

Miriam Mapetla said, 'Ah well, because you want to live what can you do? It's alright, though the money is little. I have no money since I left my husband. I never used to grumble because I am working — if I don't work, I will sleep with hunger.'

And Pauline Ndala, 'I must stay where I am ...It's no good to go in and out. You may not find another job.'

These features of working life at Knitmore — low wages, poor conditions, pressure of work, fear of losing the job — are the common experience of most African women in industry, shops or in other services.

Perhaps the machines in the textile industry impose a more relentless pace than in some other areas. But the basic problems are that women workers are vulnerable. They have few job opportunities, they need money to bring up children, they are forced to accept lower wages than men, and are not protected by the law.

FOOTNOTE:
(1) Gazette No R342: Clothing Industry (Tvl) Main Agreement, 2 March 1984.

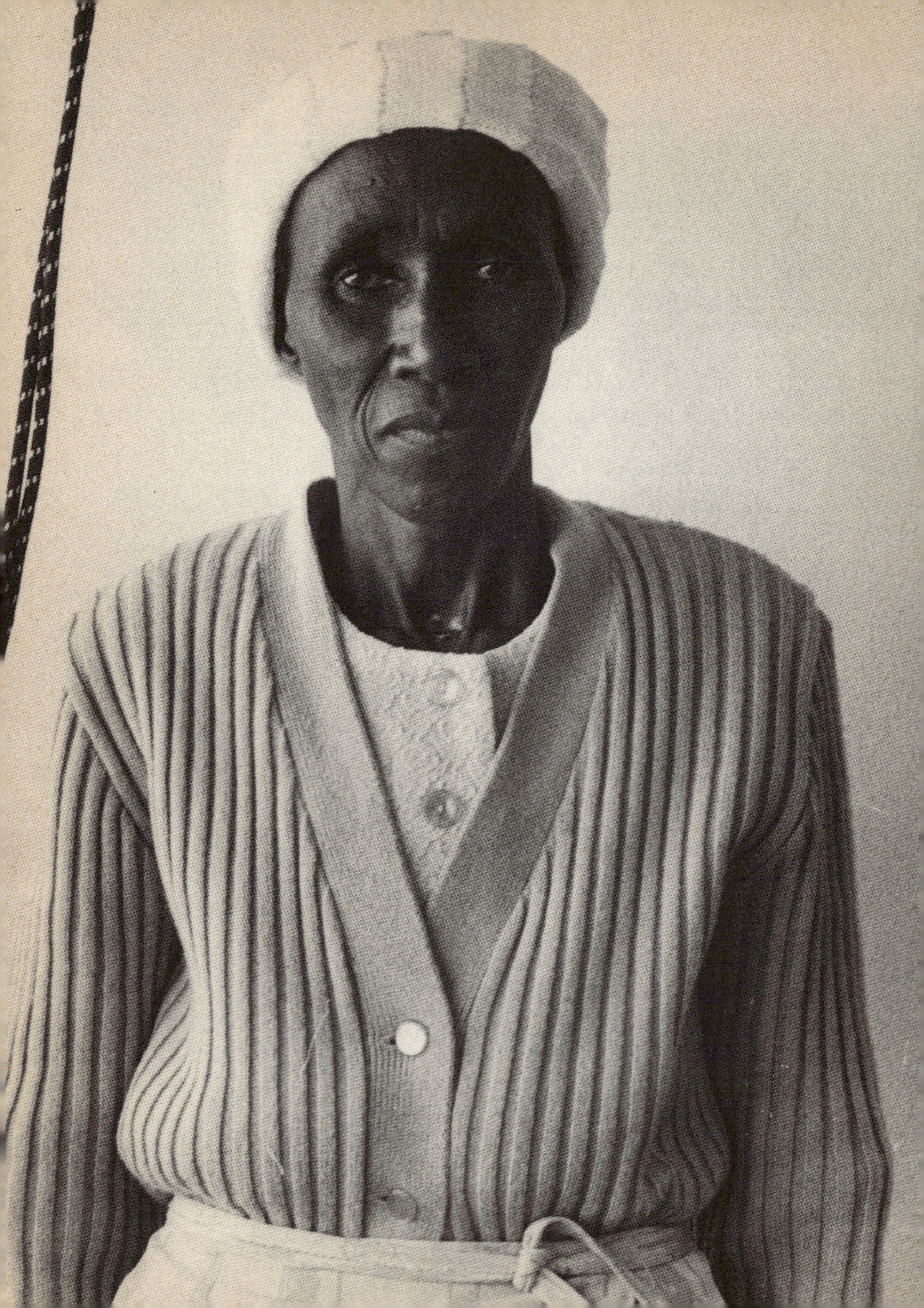

While The City Sleeps

While the city sleeps, behind the muted lights in towering office blocks, hundreds of African women work, preparing the city for tomorrow's deluge of office staff.

They scrub floors, polish desks, empty waste bins, sweep carpets. Many of these women work a full 12 hour shift, with only a short break. Often they only see their families on weekends. They usually don't get enough sleep.

The Factories, Machinery and Building Work Act of 1941 prohibited night work between 6pm and 6am for women. But factories could get exemption from this provision if they wished. Overtime was limited to a maximum of two hours a day for not more than three days in a row and not more than 60 days in a year. 'Exceptional cases' were loosely defined, so that employers could be granted exemption even in cases where there was no clear reason for doing so.

The Wiehahn Commission into labour legislation in 1979 recommended that this protective legislation be removed. The government white paper responded:

'In view of the necessity for the optimal utilization of manpower and in order to remove any differentiation on the basis of sex, the prohibition in the Factories Machinery and

Building Work Act, 1964, on the employment of women on night work after 18h00 will be repealed ... The circumstances which led to the introduction of these protective measures decades ago have in the meantime changed to the extent that such protection is no longer necessary.'

The 'circumstances' of two jobs, inadequate and expensive transportation, crime in the streets and lack of child care facilities have hardly changed. The main aim in changing these regulations was to rationalise employment practices. The effects this has on individual women is forgotten.

In the Basic Conditions of Employment Act, 1983, both men and women can now work overtime — to a maximum of ten hours a week and three hours a day. The government called this 'doing away with sexual discrimination'. But the government has simply extended provisions for the extreme exploitation of male workers to female workers.

If the government really wanted to scrap discrimination, why were men not placed under the same protective legislation which women used to enjoy?

There are countries in the world where such general prohibitions exist. In Belgium and the Netherlands night shift is completely banned for both men and women workers, except for industries which are considered essential for technological or social reasons. In France, Great Britain, and Germany night work is banned for women and children, unless exemptions are granted.

No sleep, bad health, unhappy life.

The Transport and General Workers Union conducted a small survey amongst unionised employees in a large property company in Johannesburg as background to a demand for a nightshift allowance. Some devastating facts emerged. A sample of 17 women were interviewed, with the following results.

Four of the women interviewed get only two or three hours sleep a day. Seven get three or four hours sleep a day. The rest sleep for four to seven hours a day. 'We have restless sleep, and wake up often. It is too noisy in the township to sleep properly during the day.'

Most of them had sore eyes. Some also complained that their eyesight was getting worse. This was a result of working under fluorescent lights and a lack of sleep.

Headaches were related to eye problems. Some thought they got headaches from the machines they use.

All those who said they had high blood pressure were being

treated for the problem. It was difficult to tell from the interviews whether the problem was a result of the work or not.

They complained of sore and running stomachs. Research elsewhere in the world shows exactly the same problem amongst night workers. Evidence suggests that this is related to abnormal eating patterns, and to the hours of work which interrupt any normal digestive patterns.

When the women had less sleep, they had more health problems. Every one who slept for two or three hours a day complained of stomach problems, headaches and high blood pressure.

All the women interviewed found it difficult to live a normal life. Most said their hours of work make it more difficult to attend union meetings.

'It is more difficult to do the shopping, and we can't spend time with the family, and it is very difficult to visit friends.'

'We drink tea or coffee to stay awake at night. Others take snuff. Many often take tablets such as aspirin, codis, and anadin.'

Nearly all of them said they were the only earners in the household. Nearly all said they were doing night work because they had no choice. They complained of the lack of transport facilities, and of the dangers of travelling in the early hours of the morning. Some wait for three or four hours after work before public transport is available, or before they feel it is safe to return to the township.

For these women there is nowhere to sleep and few of their buildings have cooking facilities. A few of the women manage to catch some sleep after finishing work. But they sleep on pieces of cardboard in cold, sparsely furnished change-rooms.

Chapter 3

LAST IN THE JOB QUEUE

Paul Weinberg

Farm workers are amongst the most exploited of all South Africa's workers. They include increasing numbers of women. High rural unemployment, unreliable remittances from migrant men, and no land, force them into this work.

Farm Work for Life

Farm labourers, together with domestic workers, are the most exploited of all South Africa's workers. They have few rights, and almost no legal protection against the harsh conditions, starvation wages and often the brutality of their bosses.

Yet working for low wages on a white owned farm is the lot of millions of South Africans. And amongst them are increasing numbers of women. They have little choice, for high rural unemployment, unreliable remittances from migrant men, and no land, force them into this work.

Many women farm-workers are migrants, employed on a daily or seasonal basis. Others live permanently on the farm. They are employed as domestic or casual labour, especially during the picking and harvesting times. Women are also gradually taking over jobs which men used to do. For example, women now work in dairies, on chicken farms and drive tractors.

The state has tried to channel workers onto white farms. But influx control has not been able to create a stable labour force. Conditions on most farms are very bad and labourers have often left at the first opportunity. So farmers have an untrained, unstable and erratic group of workers.

But the pass laws do have some effect. When a farm worker has a stamp in her pass to do farm work, she is confined to farm work for the rest of her life.

Wages and conditions

The real wages and living conditions of farm workers, male and female, have deteriorated over the last 20 years. Most workers are paid partly in cash and partly in kind (for example a bag of maize). Government figures give the average monthly wages of full time workers in various areas in 1980 as follows:

Average monthly wages - farmworkers

	Cash wage (R)	Value of wage in kind (R)
Eastern Orange Free State (OFS)	26.50	31.98
Western Transvaal	33.60	34.26
Northwest OFS	33.51	49.99
Highveld	26.42	50.87
Western Cape I	53.42	76.35
Western Cape II (Reuns)	79.08	67.24

But independent surveys have revealed wages far lower than these. Women are paid much less than men for doing the same work. Casual or seasonal labourers are paid less than full-time workers. In the Moiketsi area in the Northern Transvaal, women and children often work on tomato farms for no other pay than tomatoes. In 1980 in the Mathibeskraal area in Lebowa, women seasonal workers on the cotton and citrus estates earned between 30c and 80c a day and had no income out of season.

On average, women farm-workers work for 60 to 70 hours a week. There is no limit to the time they may have to work without a break, with no overtime pay.

Some farm labourers get paid annual leave, some get unpaid leave, some get no leave at all. In some places, employers decide if they will give workers any sick leave.

Assault on farm workers by their farmer bosses is not uncommon. Farm machinery accidents and poisoning by agricultural chemicals are always a hazard, and farmers discourage claims for compensation.

In some cases, especially with casual labour, women with children who can work will be employed before women with no children. The children are not paid extra.

Farm workers — in a weak position

There are many reasons for these poor conditions. Pass laws and the lack of land and jobs in the bantustans mean that there are many workers wanting jobs. Casual workers are easily sacked if they cause trouble. Farm workers are also specifically excluded from many of the laws introduced to protect industrial workers.

The recent drought and the resultant agricultural crisis has meant that, more than ever, farmers control workers' accommodation, as well as jobs.

Farm workers in the Eastern Cape.

Bee Berman

Farm Work

Many farm workers were born or grew up on white-owned farms. Yet if their contract of employment ends, they lose their right to stay. This is especially serious for women with children. The threat is real.

Between 1960 and 1970 about a million people were moved off the white-owned farms as a result of laws abolishing squatting and labour tenancy. It is no surprise that, for fear of eviction, the old and infirm often continue to work past pensionable age. Workers are afraid of victimisation if they attempt to organise in a trade union.

On average, women farm-workers work for 60 to 70 hours a week. There is no limit to the time they may have to work without a break with no overtime pay.

Cedric Nunn

Farm Work

The Orange Vaal General Workers Union has begun to organise farm labourers. Its members work on corporation owned farms in the Vaal area. The Food and Canning Workers Union also organises farm workers. But as yet, only a very small percentage of farm workers have had any contact with trade unions.

Many workers have been pushed off the farms. This means that farm labourers will often accept appalling conditions in the knowledge that a job of any kind is better than none at all.

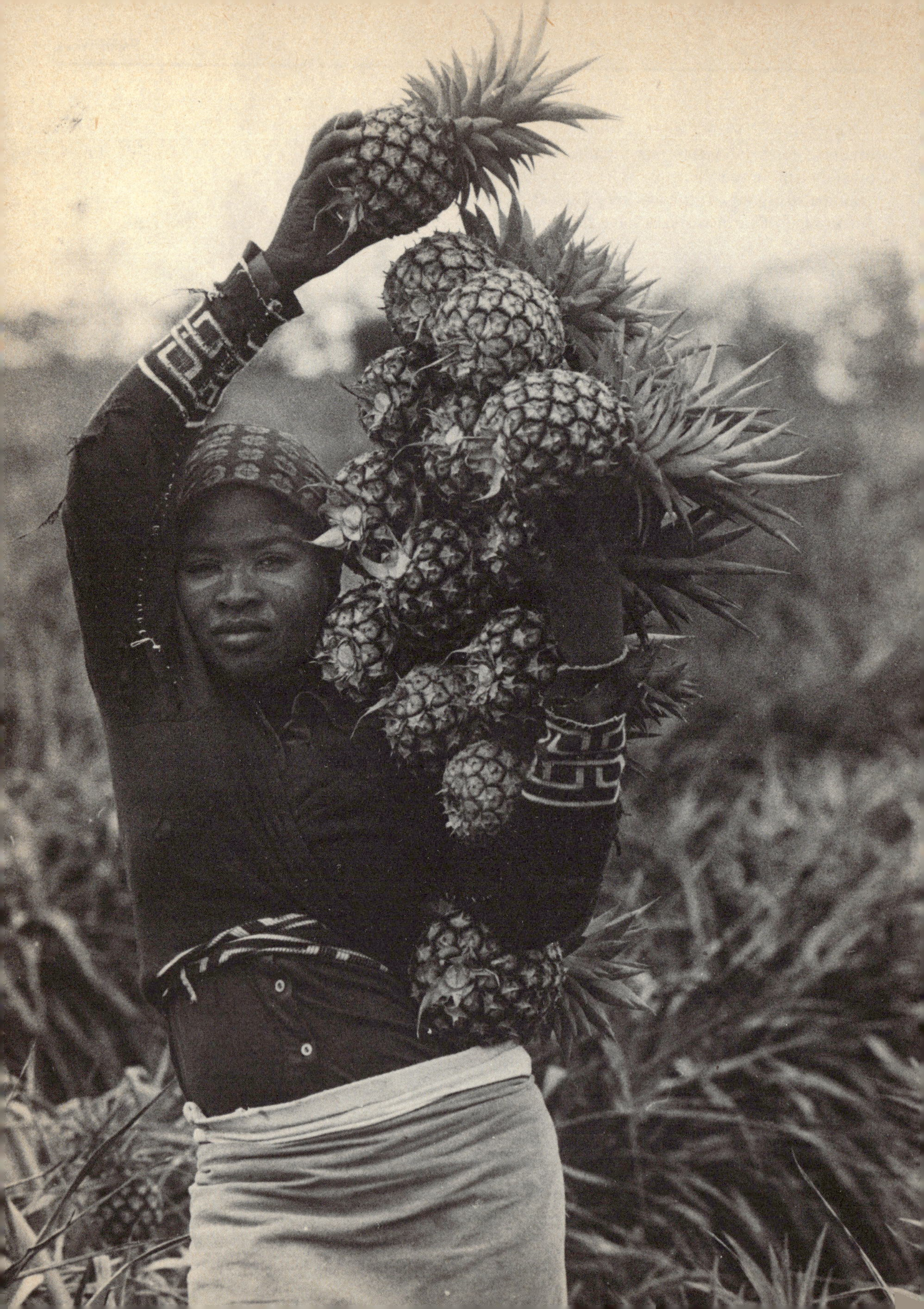

Working On A Factory Farm

Over 30 casual workers join the permanent workforce on a large factory farm in Orange Free State (OFS) during the harvest season. They pick and can the crop. These workers came mainly from three areas, Qwa Qwa, the Herschel district of the Transkei and Onverwacht, a black resettlement area in the OFS.

More than two thirds of this seasonal workforce are women. This work is the only employment they have. Because of influx control they cannot work in the cities, although some have had illegal jobs in towns for short periods. The canned products from this farm are mainly for export to Europe.

The interview which follows is with an elderly woman who worked in the canning section of the farm during the 1983 season. The farm will not be identified to protect the worker interviewed. The interview was conducted three days after she returned to her home village of Sterkspruit in the Transkei at the end of the contract.

The hostel

'The conditions are very bad. We have made these wooden pallets to sleep on because there are no beds. There are some bunk metal beds in other hostels but these we have made for ourselves. There is no place to wash, no shower. We all bought these basins to wash in.

'There is no water from the tap in each hall and outside also. The outside water is very dirty, it is from the dam. When the water inside was finished we drank that dam water even though we were not allowed to, but what could we drink?'

Women workers

'There are mainly women in the factory. There are a few men who work at the big pots cooking asparagus — about seven men. The women work in the sections packing the full tins onto the pallets and moving them. The workers in the fields have it better, they start at six o'clock and every day they knock off at three o'clock. Their food is taken to them on tractors.

'But we just work right through. We get half an hour each for breakfast and lunch. When we work at night we get a break to eat at six. Sometimes we come out at ten or eleven o'clock.

'If we got that money weekly it would be alright but we are paid monthly. And when I saw this pay I said "this is robbery". We don't all earn the same. Between R48 and R53 a month. They promised me R60 a month but they did not say that we would have to work in this way. They said everything was there for us, a kitchen, places to sleep and everything nice. But when we ask about more money for extra time they say they pay us to clock when we have clocked in. But often we have clocked in very very early and left late.

'I was contracted to work here by Rantsane in Sterkspruit. He is a black person with an office near here. He earns nicely because he earns on account of us.

'Most of us here say that we won't go back home because the work is here. I can't think of going back to Transkei. But I would like to have another contract job.

'It's not such hardship to go to the maize harvest. If you are sick there the employer takes you to a doctor. I think you do get less money at the maize but you get bags of maize, you eat well there — maize and potatoes and beans. People who work at the maize earn according to how many bags they harvest. It depends on your own strength. Also an animal is slaughtered every week so you get some meat there.

'People also say that you eat well at the potato harvest. A lot of food. Another job is harvesting cabbages. It is said that is a difficult job. But some say the money is alright, others say there is no money.'

Food

'We buy food from the store on the farm. The prices are the same as in a shop. We had to buy food because the food they gave to us in the farm factory was just pap. Everybody knows that you need to change food and you must eat fish or meat or bread as well as pap. The pap they gave to us was dirty and coarse and smelling. Men were hired to cook that pap for us. It couldn't be cooked by women because it was in those big pots and was very heavy so only men could stir it.

'We only get food if we go to work. There is no food at the hostel. We don't get any tea with pap. Sometimes we get soup. On Wednesdays we get one chicken foot, one "nggina" not even scraped. I told them not to serve one for me. An old lady like me can't eat that. On Fridays we get a small piece of cow's meat.'

Illness and injury

'If you are ill they won't even ask how you are or what's wrong. You just have to look after yourself if you are sick. And you have to pay a fine of one rand a day for every day that you are sick. There is a sort of clinic on the farm but no doctor or nurse. If you go there what do they give you? Only Engelse sout [epsom salt] if you have a stomach problem, and if you hurt yourself they anoint it.

'There have been some people injured at work. One young girl, tins fell on her and she went to hospital. I don't know if they paid her or if they deducted money from her wages. She recovered and came back to work here but I don't know where she is now, there are so many of us here in the hostel.

'Sometimes the white people beat you. If you drop a tin, they can beat you for just that one tin. One girl was beaten by a white man for dropping a tin. He pushed her this way and that way. Then some other men who were working there amongst the tins intervened to protect her. We went on strike that day.

'But other people have been beaten before that. There was a young boy in the kitchen who was beaten for no reason. But he was not really injured.

'There was this other one who was really badly hurt. He worked in the fields as a foreman. He was just sitting there and this white man kicked him. That young man ran away and he thought he was just playing. The white man chased him and he went and told the other whites and they came and took him to the office.

'After they came out of that small office they had blood all over their shirts. The young man was red, blood coming out of his nose and from his mouth and his ears. We took him to the hospital, we would not let the supervisor take him to the hospital. And we found an attorney for him there in town. I am not sure what happened, the people from his home who took him will know.'

The strikes

'We have complained about the food here, the pap, that it was not cooked properly. A white man would turn off the steam and it would be raw. As soon as the barrel of mealie meal began to boil he'd turn the steam off and the pap didn't cook. We said we were not going to work. Then they took it out and cooked new pap, and all the time we sat and did not work. We only went in about three hours later when we had eaten the cooked porridge.

'Another time we didn't want to speak to the white boss. We just said we're not going to work. We asked, "Why are our children being beaten? Why did you hit this child, how many is it now, is it not the third person you have hit today?" The big boss Henry came and he said he did not know about people being beaten here.

'The third time we went on strike it was about there being no overtime pay. At eight o'clock we said, we are leaving now. They played with us. They spoke to us and they called the big boss. All this time we weren't working. The boss said, "I don't know anything about not paying overtime. I'll pay you overtime. You all go and do your work. What am I to do if you stop work and the work isn't finished and you say you are leaving."

'We have been on strike five times over all these things but they are still not right. You can see here on the pay-slip that we still do not get pay for overtime and the money for ordinary time is low anyway.'

Anna Mazibuko

There You Are Under The Cows

Anna Mazibuko is 41 years old. She lives in Driefontein, an area in the Eastern Transvaal which is threatened with removal in terms of government resettlement policy. She has lived in Driefontein since 1983. She lives with an old woman whom she refers to as her grandmother. The two women, who have the same surname and may be distantly related, discovered each other at a time when Anna was in desperate need of a home, and when the old woman was lonely and in search of company.

Anna's story reflects the rootless existence that many women born in white farming areas are forced to live. She shifted between work on farms and work in white kitchens. Always insecure, she moved from job to job in the search for more money for her children. The search finally led to Driefontein — where the prospects of employment are nil...

Farms and Kitchens

'The first place I worked was on the farms. I worked in Amesfoort [South Eastern Transvaal] in the yard of Jan Niekerk. I was 12 years old and my job was to look after the children of the nonatjie — his wife. But at that time I didn't earn any money. I just worked for a plate of food.

'Then my family moved to Morgenzon in the Eastern Transvaal. It is near Standerton. I was 14 then. I worked on a farm and we used to plough there. We didn't earn wages then. That was the time when you got some of the crop, but there was no crop that year, so we moved after six months. There was no crop because there was no rain.

'I ran away from the farms and went to the town of Morgenzon and worked for a doctor. I earned R3 a month. I left that job because the missus was very mean. I was then 15 years old.

'So I went to look for work with other whites and found a job with a woman. But she was very poor. Her floors were made from cow dung. She paid me five shillings a month. But she made me a pretty dress so I had something to wear. She made it with her own hands.

'But I only stayed four months and then I went to some others called Groenewald. There I did everything — wash, cook, clean the house. There I earned R3 a month. I stayed there for six months and I left and went off again.

'So then I went to Holmdene [Eastern Transvaal] and stayed with my sister on a farm. That man's name was Swanepoel. I was paid R4 a month doing lots of different jobs. I was expected to work as hard as an adult but very quickly. I had to weed, thresh the mielies, and bind the mielies into bundles. I really worked there. For every sack of mielies I got five cents. It had to be absolutely full, and white inside.

'In the farms you work very hard — even today people still work like that. I lived with my sister in Holmdene for a year. The boss we were working for left and so we went to Standerton when the family home moved there from Morgenzon. This was after my father died.

'I lived in Standerton with my brothers for a while. I worked for Mr Viljoen who is now a very important man in Pretoria. He is now called Doctor Viljoen. He was the superintendent of the township in Standerton. Then he went to Ermelo, and then to Nelspruit. He was the superintendent and so his job was to smash down the townships and make them pretty. He spoke very good Zulu. He had four children, but I've forgotten their names. I used to look after them.

'He demolished Ermelo location and made Phumule. And in Standerton he demolished all our tin houses and made "Losmachine". In this way he progressed eventually to Pretoria.

Paul Weinberg

Farms and Kitchens

'He was never a doctor of bodies. He was a doctor of demolition. He's got old now. I used to wash and clean and cook. I earned R8 a month from Mr Viljoen. In that time everything went according to permission. I didn't have permission from the farm I was born on to work in the town. Dr Viljoen fixed me up and got the permission.

'After Dr Viljoen I worked for another household. But that woman was impossible. She was really kwaai [angry]. So I left there. I ran away. I ran away from a lot of places. I'm not prepared to work for whites who make me cross.

'So then I worked for another boss in Standerton — also earning R8 a month. I left that place properly, because my permission had expired. So I left and went back home.

'When I went home I had a baby. She only lived for one year and a month. She died. So I left.

'I decided it was the time to get married, so I set off to find a man. The one I found was no good, but I had many of his children. I had nine, but five died. I still have four children. They were all the children of the man I married. Three of them were boys.

'That man was from Standerton. He's from the farms, and he's there until today. I couldn't agree with him so I left. Last week I went to look for my children. I found the youngest who is ten. The only one I have with me is my daughter. The three boys are with him. I am separated now from that man. But I said to him he should keep the children, because I knew when I left I'd be very poor.

'Life on the farms is very hard. It's very heavy. In Standerton where I lived with the father of my children we would get up at six in the morning. The woman of the family (that is I), would have to start cooking and the man would have to start milking. Even now he's still milking at six.

'After cooking for the children and my husband I would go to the farmhouse and do the cooking and cleaning. I earned R12 a month — working for Mr Human and his wife and daughter-in-law.

'At the farms there's a lot of ploughing. If it does not rain you're in a lot of trouble. My husband has always earned R30 a month and a bag of meal. And he would get the corners of the fields (the agterskot), after the reaping. So if the crop died you died.

'The white farmer never gave us extra. And yet he knew my husband was a man with a wife and children. In the years when there was no rain, those were the years when our children died.

'My husband used to have two cattle. I am not sure if he still has them.

'He had three wives. The first one left in 1969. She couldn't bear it. The first wife lasted for eight years. I stayed for 17 years.

Gill de Vlieg

Fetching water at Driefontein.

Farms and Kitchens

I realised I could never bear the way of life on the farms. I'd rather work for R40 a month and know that I'll get clothes and food. But there you never know.

'Even now that man is still milking at six o'clock. Every afternoon at 4pm he calls them in again to the shed and sits down beneath them and starts again to milk. That's the law of the whites. Whatever the weather, wherever you are. There you are under the cows.

'In the morning after the milking he must go out and plough the fields on the tractor, skoffel [weed and hoe the fields], start again to plough the fields, skoffel the fields ... and at four o'clock he must get off the tractor and get under the cows.

'Next morning same thing. Then when you've finished ploughing and skoffeling, back to the cows. After you've milked the cows you must go to make cream on the machine. And after the cream he can go home. That was his life. Day in and day out.

'As for me, my life was a white lady's kitchen — day in and day out. All for that R12.

'There were only two black households on the farm. That

Approaching Driefontein.

Paul Weinberg

boss was dirt poor. His father died and he had to take over the farm. Before that he lived in a caravan, going from place to place with his children. When he got here to the farm he found us already here.

'That first year we certainly ploughed. We got 1800 bags, as well as sunflower seeds. That's where he got the money to buy the tractor.

'I left in 1979 on the 6th January. When I went I left another woman behind. That was his last wife. I left my children because I could see no other way out of it.

'My husband gave me R10 a month. I was supposed to buy everything for my children and myself. I couldn't manage. So I said good-bye. In the same way his first wife left him. And we left the young wife. But she'll also leave. She's got four children. But she'll leave too. In the six years the new wife was there she had four children. Only one died.

'Last week I went to see my children. They are really suffering now. At least when I was there I used to buy some things with the kitchen money. I used to get second hand clothes from whites. Now that I'm not working there's nothing I can do for them. At the time when I was working I used to send them clothes at Christmas.

'I sit at home because I can't get registered, and they suffer. Because they have no shoes and they have to walk to school their feet are cracked. That is the greatest poverty of my life — my children. But the eldest is alright. He's now working at Bronkhorstspruit. He got a job in Standerton with LTA, a construction company, and was transferred to Bronkhorstspruit. I went to try to find him to ask for money but I couldn't find him.

'When I left my husband I went to look for a job and I found one in Piet Retief in the Eastern Transvaal, working in the houses of men who were making the dam. In Piet Retief they refused to register me. This was in 1982.

'I worked for one woman for nine months. During that time the police arrested me and locked me up again and again. My missus would get me out.

'They kept saying I must go back to Standerton. I kept saying, back to what in Standerton? — I have no mother, no father. My father died in 1962 and my mother in 1982. And so I had to leave and I began to search for a place. So I went to look for my grandmother.

'So I came to Driefontein. I thought I could find a place to live, which I could have as an address and get registered. By luck I found my grandmother. I now live with her. I've been here for a year now.

'But the problem is I still can't get a contract and permission to work. So we haven't got money. I am really struggling. Now

Farms and Kitchens

I'm really platsak [broke] because I went to visit my children and that finished me. If I could just get registered I could get a job easily, because there are jobs.

'There is only one in the family who is alright now. That is my one sister who now lives in Soweto and is married. There were ten of us, and eight lived. The rest of us are not married anymore. We have all really suffered. One sister lives in Standerton and she's got a house. But she has no children. She has nobody. Her two children died.

'My other sister is still in the kitchens in Standerton. She managed to bribe a pass. She bought a pass. So she's working. You can buy it from any white who will write a letter to say you were born on his farm and left it.

'But you get caught. Many of the whites have already been caught. Because once they've caught the white he betrays you. Then they put you in jail. There are lots of people who have tried it and some have succeeded. When you get evicted from Standerton you get evicted to KwaNdebele [bantustan north of Pretoria].

'What happened to my father in the end was that his young wife had a lover, and she and her lover killed him and left him in the forest.

'When we heard he had died I knew that was the end. Before that I always used to think that no matter how poor I was I could go back to my father. His place on the farm is now lost. His father was born there, and his father's father. My father's wife's lover was arrested because he was found with my father's pass. The case was heard in Standerton and he got seven years.

'Yes, I've had a hard life. It all started because my father deserted my mother in 1948 when I was seven years old. My father got another young wife and my mother went off with me and my brother.

'It was because of that we had to work. She really suffered for us. Working in the kitchens was a new thing. In those days we used to get mielie meal and eggs and would trade for sugar and things.

'In the time that I lived with my mother I thought and thought of a way to change things. I came up with getting married. I thought by getting married I would get my own place. So I tried it and it was terrible. So I left. And until today I've never solved that problem.

'So today I'm living here with my grandmother - the mother of one of the many brothers in my father's family.

'My main problem is still the pass. What I want is permission to work anywhere — not just in Piet Retief or somewhere. In Wakkerstroom if you can get a pass you can work in Jo'burg or Sasol — of course you can't go to Natal, but Jo'burg is good enough.'

Only A Few Chickens

In rural South Africa, many people earn as little as R100 a year. In KwaZulu in 1983, for example, the average income of women was only R74 per year.

Few people have any land, and resources like fuel and water are scarce. Chiefs and administrators earn comfortably, but they hand out favours to some and ignore the needs of the majority.

Most women struggle to eke out an existence without any reliable income, and often without the help of men. Rural people also pay a great deal of tax in relation to their income. Many older people will say that life in the rural areas has not always been as bad as it is now.

An old woman in the Northern Transvaal said, 'We used to have 20 morgen before the land was cut. Then we got 50 to 60 bags of mealies and also beans. We used to sell. Now the land is cut there is only one morgen and all there is is one or two bags of maize.'

This is a common story, echoed by many of the people living on barren and drought stricken land.

Ma Sara Masemola lives in a village in the Northern Transvaal just outside Pietersburg. She explained how she managed to keep her household going, 'I have no ploughing land and no stock. Only a few chickens. I try to grow mielies around my house. But it is smaller than a morgen and I get almost nothing.

'So I make beer and sell it. I get a profit of R4 every weekend.

Gill de Vlieg

It costs me R2 to make the beer. My husband also gives me R9 a week for food. He earns R20 and pays R2 on transport to work. This place is expensive. We had to pay the chief R11 when we came. Then another R1 for the yard and R2 for the levy, and R2 for tax. We also had to pay R12 for the van to get here.'

Many people are unemployed in these remote areas. In recent years people living in urban areas have been given preference for jobs. Rural people fall into the job queue last. For women it is even worse. Men can sometimes be recruited as contract labourers. But women are not recruited at all.

Pensions are often the only source of income for people in rural areas. But inefficient and corrupt administration often means that old and sick people are denied their legal right to claim pensions.

In many areas people have to sign for pensions before they are given money. In other areas people must bribe officials to consider their applications. Many old people say that they are told to, 'find a lover', or 'ask your children for money', when they try to apply for their pensions.

Many women try to support themselves by making goods to sell, or re-selling goods they have bought in towns. A fruit seller in Winterveld, a resettlement area just outside Pretoria, supports her mother-in-law, her own three children and three orphans. She is a widow. Because she has no pass, she cannot get legal work. So the only means of making money is to sell fruit.

'We buy these peaches from the market and sell them to make a living. We are selling them at 2c each and at a profit of R2, after having bought the stuff for R1. This profit is earned after two days. [This gives her an income of R30 per month.] At times we have nothing to eat. At times then, when I have old porridge I mix it with water and I give this to the children so that they have something in their stomachs.'

The vegetables and fruit that these women sell are usually the 'leftovers' from the Pretoria market. The fruit has to be fetched by truck and the women must pay for this. The poor quality of the produce means they have to sell at low prices. The women usually cannot get traders' licences, so they are vulnerable to arrest.

For many women the last steady job they had was many years ago. But still they say that they are 'looking for work'.

'The last time I worked was in 1968. We worked in the quarry picking up kalk stones. I worked together with my daughter-in-law. We earned R10 a month each. The work was from 6am to 6pm with no break. But then the job finished. Now I am looking for kitchen work. I weave and knit to sell. It makes about R60 a year.'

Rural people fall into the job queue last. For women it is even worse. Men can sometimes be recruited as contract labourers. But women are not recruited at all.

Omar Badsha

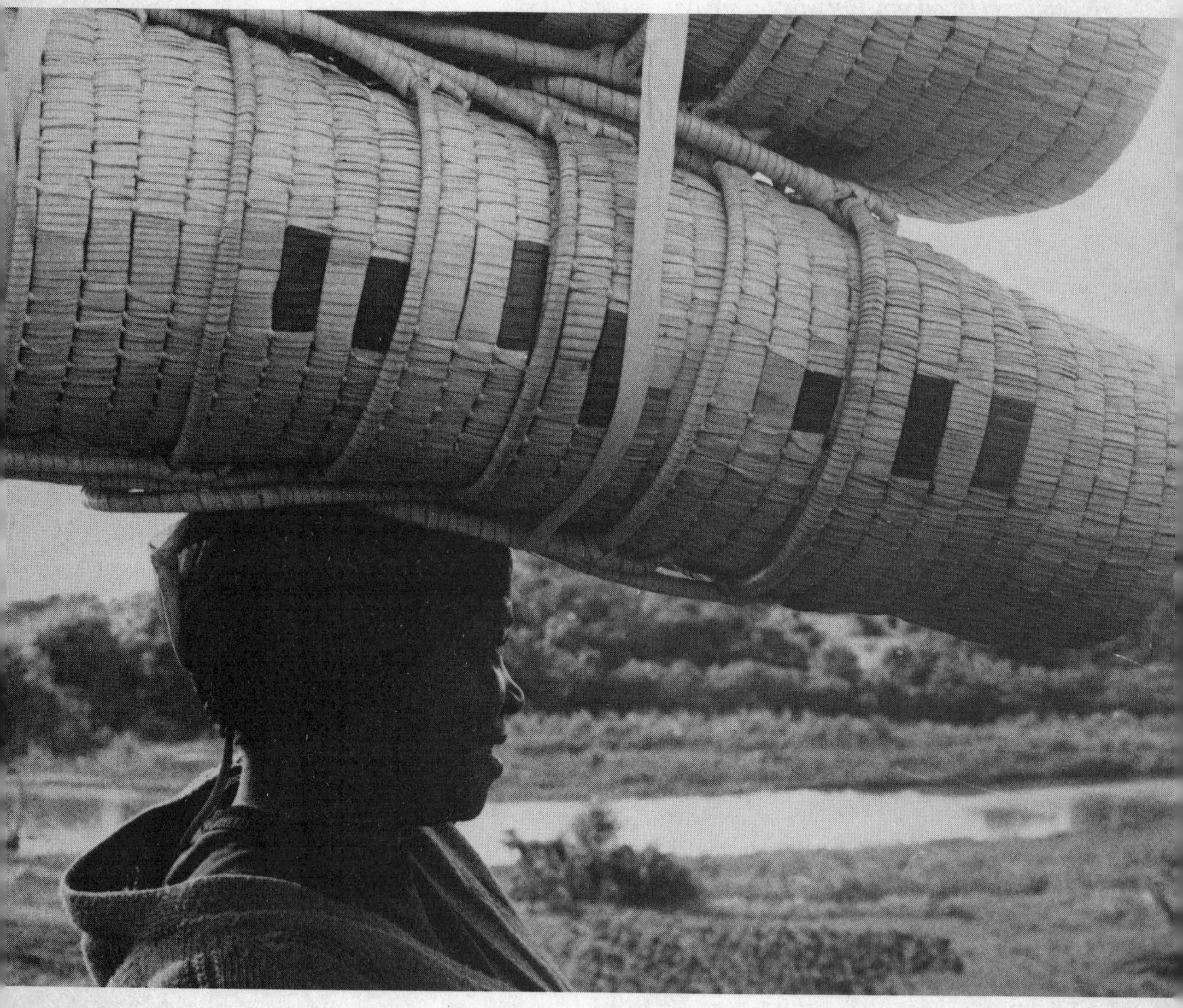

And How Will We Survive?

Between the security of a regular job and the despair of total unemployment is the informal sector. People earn their living by sewing, buying and selling, or running shebeens.

Many unemployed women drift into informal sector activities. At first it is a stop-gap while they are still looking for jobs. Then, as the search becomes more difficult, the informal sector becomes a permanent way of earning money.

The informal sector is often romanticised. The virtues of enterprise and hard work and the ideal of the 'self-made man' have been held up as the results of informal sector activity.

Nafcoc's (National African Federated Chambers of Commerce) attempt to foster small business development, and the recent recommendations in the commission of inquiry into the Ciskei all see informal sector activities as one of the solutions to the lack of jobs. But only a few reach the top.

For unemployed and often elderly women the informal sector offers very little. The following people show vividly the great effort that provides small rewards.

Jemima Dose said, 'I make money by selling beers. A dozen costs R8-10 and I normally buy four dozen. Each is sold at 90c. I use a refrigerator to cool them and I buy a litre of paraffin at

A mat-maker in Sherube Village in Natal.

63c. My customers buy them and take them away. Some customers spend the day up to 8pm.

'At times we get arrested and a fine is R10, and our stock gets confiscated. There is no place where you could claim for the confiscation. I have been selling beer for four years. It is better when you work because this business is not always profitable. At times there are no customers and you might land up not having sold a thing throughout the week. The profit is R50 or R54 a week, depending on how I sold. This includes the brandy and the spirits.'

Many informal sector activities are illegal. Police harassment is a constant worry for many women.

Sarah Buthelezi, 'I make money by selling spinach and maize to the people. In order to get these I have to travel by car to the farm. A trip is R6 depending on the distance. If it is far it would be more.

'For spinach the charge is R10 or R14 a bundle. When selling I don't see any profit. Because the next time I pay in almost all from that money. I sell from an open space.

'Police used to harass us before. But of late they have stopped. I have applied for a licence. But I was told to wait until everything is fixed. I am still waiting, but I and other people have asked to be given a chance without harassment because it is not a fault of ours that the licences are never ready.

'But we must live. And how will we survive? I have been doing this on and off since 1974 when my elder daughter was still at school. It is not the best, but I can still help myself out. After all the money is deducted I make a profit of R5 a day.'

Because profits are so low the women have to account for every cent they spend.

Nancy Nhlapho said, 'I have been without a job since 1975. Now I live by selling. I usually buy a bag of cake flour at R42, fish oil at R8.50, yeast at R1.05, sugar at R14.80, snoekfish depending, at times I get a big piece at R2.10, and achaar [pickled vegetables] a tin it is R15. So for vetkoek [fried dumplings which can be stuffed with fish or meat] you need coal, wood and matches. Roughly for fuel every month it is R36.40. My total score comes up to roughly R120 every month.

'I have been doing this from 1980. It is worse than a proper job because when I was working I used to earn more than that per month. But now my health doesn't allow me to go and work.'

Sewing dresses in a backyard in Tembisa.

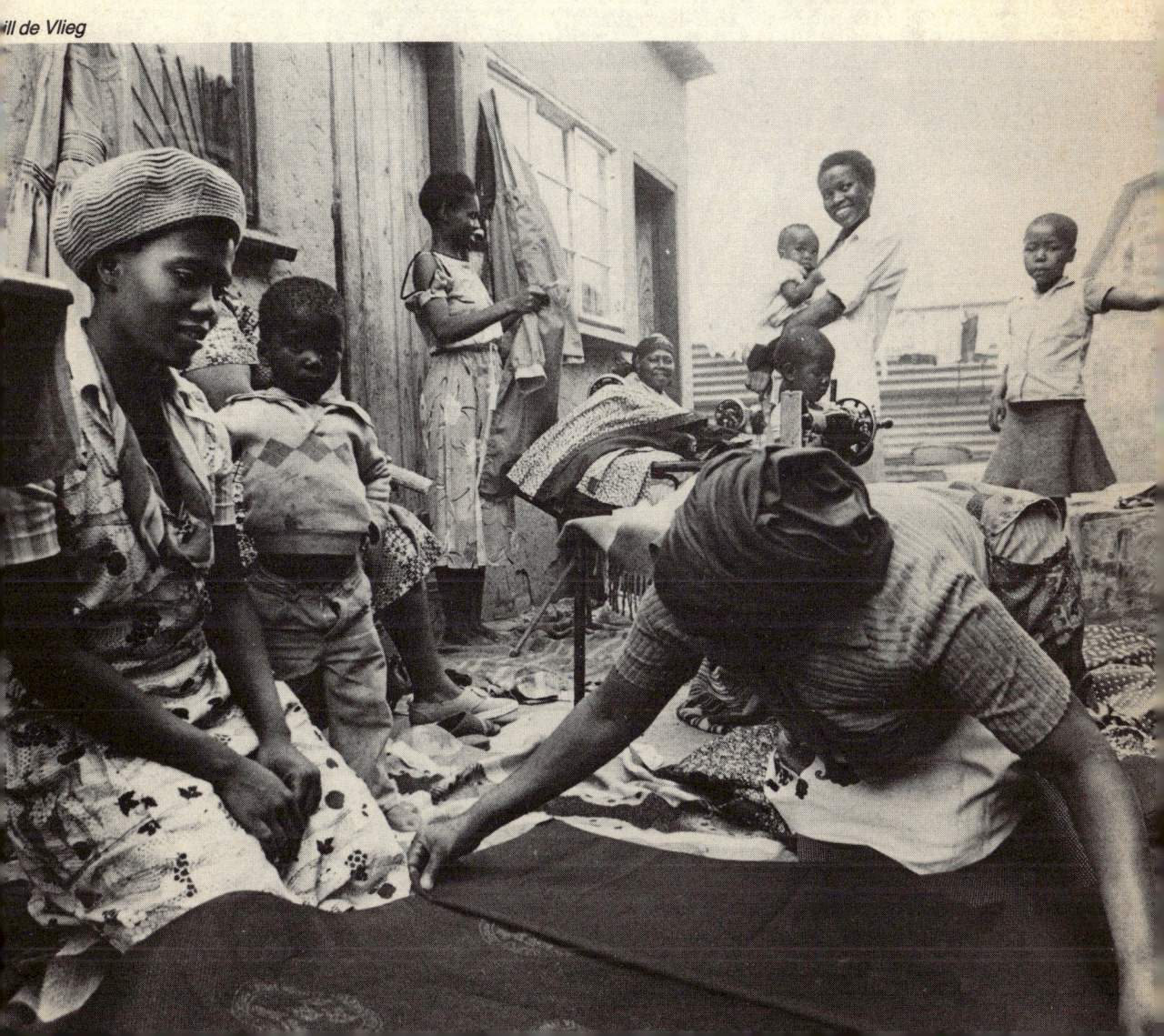

Gill de Vlieg

Other women see their informal sector work as a supplement to money that they get from other sources,

'I make money by selling pillow cases and sheets. Normally I buy for R20 and a profit would be R5 every week per stock. This has been for a period of three years. It is worse because if I spend R20 on material the R5 gain cannot come up to all my demands. But for the meantime it is not too bad because it is just an addition to what my boyfriend offers.'

No Jobs At All

For hundreds of thousands of women there are no jobs in the towns, no jobs on the farms, no jobs in the rural areas and no jobs in the bantustans. Unemployment in South Africa is here to stay. Even during times of economic growth, the number of unemployed people is always growing.

During the 1960s foreign investors began to pour money into the South African economy. But the emphasis was on technology rather than creating large numbers of jobs. The number of people working did increase, but the number of unemployed people still grew.

The rise in black unemployment in South Africa was dramatic - 1 236 000 in 1960, to 2 306 000 in 1977.

With rapidly increasing unemployment there are groups of people who are especially vulnerable. Young people, women, and those restricted to rural areas come off worst.

It is almost impossible to find accurate statistics on general unemployment in South Africa. In the case of women the task is even more difficult. The reason is that state statistics define unemployed people as those who have recently lost their jobs and are actively seeking new work. Otherwise, 'unemployment' refers to people registered at government

Omar Badsha

Unemployed in Inanda, Natal

labour bureau as work-seekers.

Unemployed people often do not register at the labour bureau because they are generally offered badly paid, heavy work. Many of them cannot register, because they may be in an urban area illegally. In rural areas many people have lost all hope of ever finding jobs through the labour bureau.

State statistics also have a category called 'not economically active'. In the 1980 census 6 473 500 out of 8 227 680 African women were classified as 'not economically active'. This is over three quarters of all African women.

But defining people as 'not economically active' hides the number of African women in South Africa who are unemployed or under-employed.

Housewives are classified as 'not economically active'. This hides the time, energy and labour that goes into looking after households. The African working class has little access to state child-care facilities. Women may often have to choose between staying home to look after children, or working and leaving them alone at home. If these facilities were easily and cheaply available, many more women would undoubtedly seek work.

Many women leave work or are fired because of ill-health. Sarah Rwexu said, 'I am unemployed. I have worked at a drycleaner. Because of a stroke in 1974 I left that job. I have been without a job for eight years.

'I felt bad leaving because I liked my job. It was a light job, despatch and receiving goods. I am looking for a job, but not far away, because I still have a problem with my left foot. I cannot move fast or for a long distance. I look for jobs by applying, but there is nothing.'

And Harriet Nakho, 'It is now close to five years that I have been out of work. I was declared redundant through illness, and though not seriously ill I had to leave work. In fact, my boss suggested that I leave work because he had a younger more energetic person to replace me.'

At the time she lost her job Harriet was 47 years old. The working life of African women is often very short.

Eunice Shabangu said, 'I am unemployed since 1979 until the present due to illness. I cannot tell exactly what is wrong with me. I feel the pains all over my body and my feet get swollen when I stand for long hours working. I have been to so many doctors, even Baragwanath Hospital [Soweto], but in vain.

'I was working at John Orr's Eloff at the cut-and-blow hairdressing salon, earning a sum of R60 per month. Due to salary dissatisfaction I went to Strijdom Hospital working as a cleaner, but there I was earning R53 per month. I was unhappy about that salary, but there was nothing I could do because I had to run a family.

'Due to illness I had to leave and go for a breast operation. It is a period of four years I have been without a job.'

This woman is now 42 years old. At 38 she became, to all intents and purposes, unemployable. The kind of job she would like shows how she sees herself in the ranks of the unemployed.

She says, 'I am looking for work. I would like to work under the West Rand Board collecting rubbish in the streets. It is hard to get a job because there are many people who are unemployed and no work in factories.'

The long search for work is a depressing experience for many women. Women work-seekers interviewed in a survey in Soweto used a number of methods. The first was to go door to door, from factory to factory and shop to shop. Many of the women found this an expensive and unsatisfactory method of finding work. The following stories are from the survey.

Elaine Jwalo said, 'I usually look for a job through asking at doors. It is hard to get a job because when you get to a place looking for a job you can never know whether that place is a right one, or maybe it could be a place where people get killed. You, the one in need, you just go in and at times the boss just says I don't need people. One has to move out disappointed because you were with the hope of being employed.'

The most common way to find work is to ask friends and relatives to look for vacancies at their workplace. Two of the women had found work in this way. Other women felt that this was unfair. They felt at a disadvantage if they did not have personal contacts in a workplace.

Brenda Magubane said, 'I have been without a job for three years. I am looking for a job. It could be in factories in Johannesburg, but I have never gone out to look. I usually ask my neighbours who work to find out for me if they are looking for people where they work.'

Going to factory gates looking for work and being turned down is very discouraging and depressing.

Matilda Mkhize, a 45 year old woman said, 'It is hard to find a job because one finds that there are many people in the lines for jobs so it is difficult to be picked up from that lot. I once went to Baragwanath hospital looking for a job as a cleaner, and was told by the superintendent that I was too old. Since then I have not looked for work.'

A last attempt at finding work is to go to the labour bureau in Polly Street in Johannesburg. Elain Jwalo said, 'I sometimes used to go to Polly, to line up and wait for the clerks to come and call you one by one. It means to be the first one you had to wake up very early and if not you didn't get anything.'

Shako Khumbane had similar experiences of the labour bureau. 'I live through marketing and I also look for a job by going to Polly. We always report in those offices at 7am and stand in a queue. The clerks will call us one by one to the office

Women street-cleaners in Soweto.
'I am looking for work. I would like to work under the West Rand Board collecting rubbish in the streets.'

if there is a job they can offer. When you are called inside you might get it, but usually not and you are unfortunate. At times we are given cards with numbers on them in rotation as they call it. It is hard because it is not easy to find a job you want through that system. It would be a question of luck.'

Esther Khumalo, 'It is hard to get a job because many factories are closing down and there are a lot of people who are looking for jobs.'

Many of the women felt guilty because they did not have a job and so could not help their families.

Shande Moloi said, 'It is now a year since I have had a job. I am actively looking for a job. Since a lot of people are unemployed I don't mind doing any kind of job. As long as I work and get something to help my husband in maintaining the children.'

Some of the women felt depressed about being unemployed.

'Unemployment has brought me loneliness and frustration. The whole day when all my family members are away at work I stay alone and there isn't enough money. So sometimes I stay without money for the whole month until my daughter comes in to give me something.'

In the bantustans women have an even harder time. There is little work and what work there is, is extremely badly paid. Many women cannot find work at all and have given up hope of ever doing so.

Official statistics define women living in rural areas as 'subsistence agricultural producers' and so they are not counted among the unemployed. But even the few people who have land usually only have about one morgen. Access to land or not, the majority of rural women are unable to exist without some form of cash income.

Like their urban sisters, once these women have had a job and lost it, it is extremely difficult to find another. Many were last employed eight or ten years ago. But they still perceive themselves as work-seekers.

Finding work is made more difficult by the restrictions of the pass laws and influx control. As Daisy Mhlope said, 'Unemployment brings three difficulties, sickness, starvation and staying without clothes.'

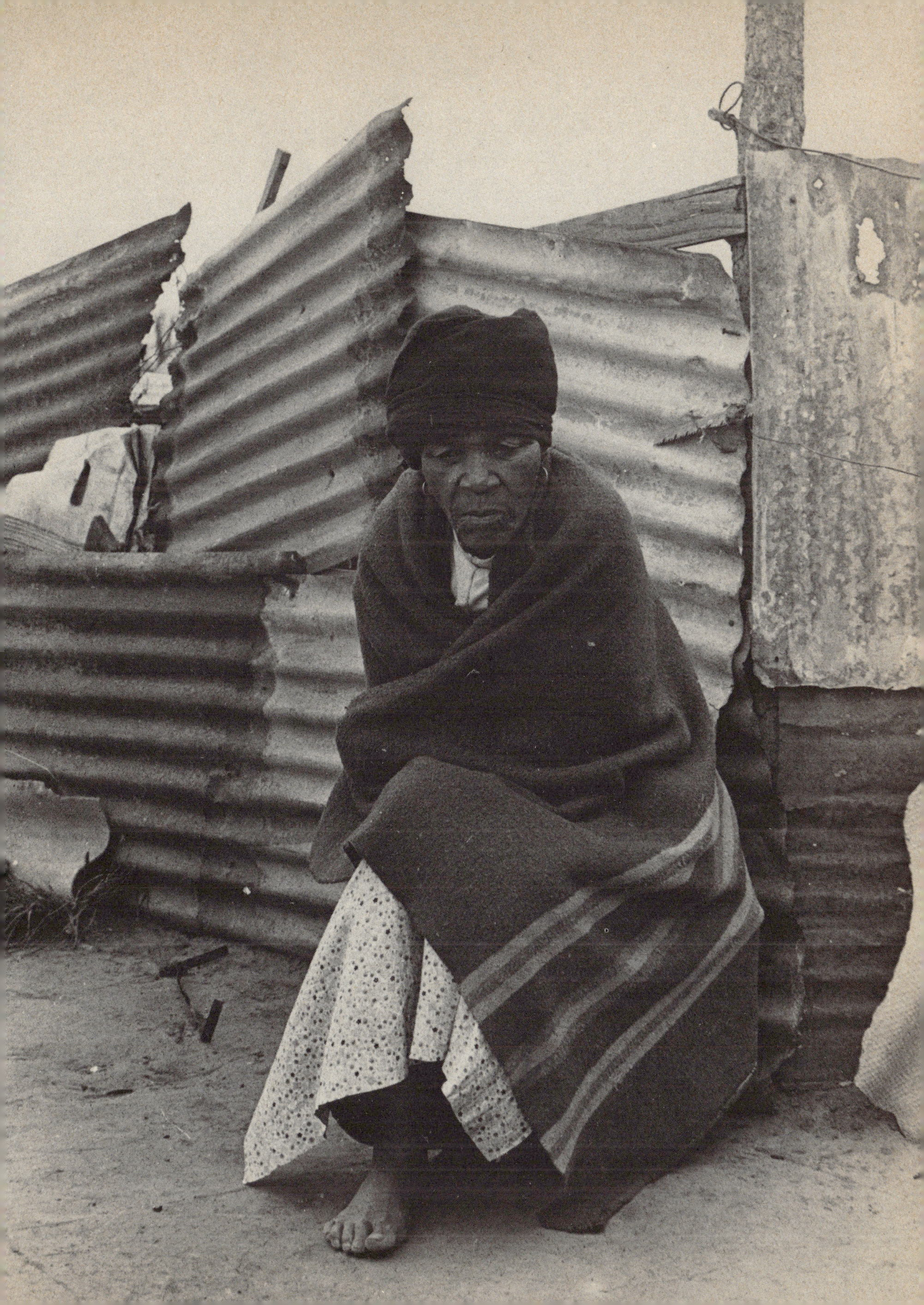

Chapter 4

UNION WOMEN

Lydia Kompe

Lesley Lawson

Lydia Kompe

Trade Unionist - Not Tea Girl

Wife, mother, trade unionist. Not the easiest combination for any woman. To be black and a woman in South Africa poses problems enough. In this account of her life, 'Mama' Lydia Kompe explains the roots of black attitudes towards men and women, and how roles are passed on to new generations — in circumcision schools, in pressure to leave school and to marry, and in the way lobola [cattle or money a man must pay to his in-laws for his new wife] is interpreted.

But 'Mama' Lydia, Transvaal Branch Secretary of the Transport and General Workers Union, is challenging traditional views of women. Her story illustrates the challenges, the defeats and the triumphs of a life committed to worker's struggle and women's struggle in South Africa.

Growing up on a mission

'I was born on 6 August 1935 at a village called Matlala near Pietersburg [Northern Transvaal]. It was a mission called the Evangelical Lutheran Church. My parents were very religious and we Christian children were not allowed to have any communication with children who belonged to another church. But it was worse with the people who didn't attend church at all. They were called heathens. It was quite difficult for us.

'We didn't have a mission school so we had to attend the tribal school where we had a lot of outside friends. We spent three-quarters of our lives with them at school. Sometimes there was a clever girl that you really loved at school, you sit with her at the same desk, you communicate well, you play well in the playgrounds. But because she's not the same religion her parents and my parents can't actually come together.'

Circumcision — defining roles

'There were many differences between us and those children. Their parents still believed in circumcisions. For every stage that you go through, as a woman, seeing your periods, there is a traditional thing. There was secrecy, dancing...we didn't know what they were doing. When it happened to a friend he would tell me, but I wouldn't tell my parents. If they knew they'd give you hard times because they know that you can be easily influenced to go to circumcision school.

'I don't know 100% because I have not been. Those who have been only tell part of it. Before, it took three or four months. Now it takes two or six weeks. Today, people don't see circumcision school as a first priority but they still believe that it must happen. Where I live it is very common, and we are very careful to prevent our children going. My daughters went to live in that area when they were quite big. So they could decide if they wanted circumcision.

'But my son was still under age when he went to live there. He was about 14 so he could be easily swayed. My daughters phoned me to say that Abraham wanted to go to circumcision school. I went to pick him up quickly. If he went to circumcision school, he would be isolated in our family like a sore thumb, because we haven't been there. His father had taken him to hospital when he was seven to be circumcised so there was no point besides that secrecy.

'We don't know what they do, maybe they just whip them

and teach them funny things about how to sleep with women. It's what I heard. This traditional ideology of not wanting to do anything in the house, I'm sure the grassroots is from the circumcision school where they have been told "a woman is a woman". Since you've been circumcised under no anaesthetic it means you're a brave man. So a woman must actually bow. When they come out they're very bold and their mothers bow to their children because they think they've won a big victory under those kind of conditions.

'Some of my women friends say that for this period they don't sleep in the veld like men. They select one village maybe next to their chief's kraal. They can go out during the day. They don't wear clothes and they put doeks around themselves and cover themselves with skin. Most of the time they're half naked, as long as they cover the private parts. What I heard is that they cut off a piece of their clitoris. For what reason I don't know. Otherwise it is just the old women teaching them the disadvantages of sleeping with men when they are young. Old people who supervise tell them how to treat their men, how dangerous it is to sleep with men because you get pregnant.

'Even after their circumcision they were supervised. Before she receives her periods she must go and open her thighs and the old woman looks through to see if the hymen is still there. If the hymen is broken then she will be whipped to tell which boy broke her. That was sort of discipline to the children not to sleep with boys before they actually get a proper person to marry. My friends didn't tell me that they cut off their clitoris. I discovered that when I worked in a hospital.'

We must get married

'Our parents were not keen to see us educated but very keen to see us married. The first priority was for all young girls to marry before they get children. Remember there were no precautions. Anyway they would never believe in those, others still don't believe in them.

'They believe that as long as you are not married you don't have to sleep with a man. They also tell the boys that you can only romance your girlfriend but you can't penetrate. You can do all sorts of things to relieve yourself, but not actually sleep with that girl until you're married. Men were told never to sleep with their girl when she is menstruating, never sleep with a pregnant girl that you didn't make pregnant. Those are the things that men emphasised to their young boys.'

Between chief and church

'My parents farmed in the mission. We had big pieces of land where my parents relied on ploughing. We were schooled from the maize and sweet potatoes that my father would sell. At that time schooling was not expensive. My mother had seven children but by that time there were only my brother and us two sisters at school. The others were big men working in Jo'burg. But all the responsibility of schooling rested on my parents. My brother just helped my father with clothes, and some other things like seeds.

'We had cows for ploughing, and we could milk them. Every member of the church was entitled to a piece of land. Besides that the chief had to recognise us as member of his tribe and he gave us a piece of land outside the mission.

'Our fathers had to go to the chief's kraal when he requested them. The chief could decide when he wanted men for a tribal gathering. All the people are part of the tribe even if they are religious. They have to obey his instructions and may have to plough his lands at times.

'The church was a great commitment. The chief recognised and respected the missionaries and he would allow the reverend to use our parents much more than him. We ploughed a big piece of land for the church. All the food that came from the land, subsidised the church funds.'

Going to school

'I started school when I was seven years old. I stayed at school until standard five. I went to standard six when I was sixteen, and had to attend confirmation classes. Once you get confirmed and pass your standard six, you're a woman and you stay at home. I pleaded with them and they allowed me to do standard seven. My parents wanted me to marry because I'd finished school.

'In 1954, when I was supposed to do standard eight my parents had no money so I didn't even attempt to do it. I loved school. We were in Sunbeams and Wayfarers. With men they called it Pathfinders. We did a lot of lively things after school. We had a lot of medals and badges. We also did athletics. I was good at running. I used to run a mile with men. I was very fit. I was the captain of basketball. We sang in choirs, going as far as Pietersburg, 25 miles away, which was a big issue. We hired a bus. Girls were vomiting all the way along! Nobody had cars, we used donkey carts.'

Leaving Home

'I stayed for three months after leaving school. I was 19 years old. I looked for a job in Potgietersrus hospital in the Northern Transvaal. It was not a training hospital but they gave me a job.

'My parents didn't want me to work. They wanted me to stay at home and wait for marriage. I spoke to my mother privately and told her that I've got someone who is promising to marry me but he is still schooling.

'My mother knew him, he was an intimate friend of my brother who worked in the mines. My mother was quite happy to hear that I was going to get married to that guy. She released me and I ran away when my father was not there. My mother said, "I will just say you absconded".

'So I waited for him to go and look after his cattle, then I went. There were trucks around the village to pick up all those poor children to go and work on the farms. So I caught the truck.

'These trucks come to our village at four o'clock in the morning. At each corner there's a group of children who couldn't go to school and they jump into the trucks to go and work, maybe for a tin of wheat a day, or maybe for a tin of potatoes. I jumped into the trucks, saying that I was going to look for job. But they saw my suitcase, so I said "No, I'm going to get a job as a domestic there at your farm", and they got me there. My cousin worked for those farmers in the kitchen and I slept there that night.

'The following morning I took the truck to Potgietersrus hospital. I decided to work in a hospital because there was no other job that I could think of. All I wanted to do was earn a little salary to survive. I didn't want to work as a domestic. I couldn't do a teachers course without a junior certificate and at that time you could have auxillary nursing without JC. I thought I would work there for a year and go to Groothoek to train but unfortunately my husband didn't want me to go and work at Groothoek which is in the Eastern Transvaal.'

Johannesburg and marriage

'I worked at the hospital for a year. In 1955 I came to Johannesburg with that guy. He approached my parents to marry me and he paid lobola. I had a baby, and in 1958 I married him. He paid 18 cattle and there were many other things that he was supposed to pay in our tradition. My mother got a travelling rug, and my father a coat and he paid the sum of R5 for slaughtering an ox that we celebrated with.

'He had to buy some clothes that show me how my in-laws want me to dress. If they want me to go bareheaded they will not bring a scarf, but if they bring a scarf and a shawl then I must cover myself when I go out to gatherings and show respect. I had a baby already and I was expecting the second one.'

Lobola

'I'm not very happy with the way lobola is interpreted, people think that by paying lobola they are buying a person to become their servant. Once you've paid lobola you're responsible for everything anybody can do in your home. But as long as you are a daughter-in-law you've got to be responsible for everything. To my view, this is part of oppressing a person. A person should be free in her house.

'It has always been like that, but before we were working it wasn't too bad because there weren't too many things to be done at a time. We didn't have a lot of additional jobs and we could share them.

'Now we are all working. I've got to do my own job, but I must get up early to please the family, boil the water for them to wash, clean the house, and clean the yard outside. When I get back from work I must also start by cooking for them, washing dishes.

'I think lobola causes excessive divorces. If I'm not happy and my husband agrees with his family naturally I get upset and I go.

'At the moment I can't refuse lobola for my daughters. I stay amongst those people and my child has actually just been paid. I couldn't say no, and the people who want to marry her can't accept a gift, it's not tradition. You must follow the procedure of a proper marriage. She's been paid R900 and three cows!

'We call the family and have a meeting. We are in two different rooms, and we've got one person to mediate the lobola, because we would demand more and they would request less, so we could come down a bit on the cows just like wages!

'I think we should stop lobola. It doesn't mean anything. In the old days, they paid lobola to bring the families together to be committed to each other. For example my family's poor and my daughter is to be married to people that have a lot of cattle. Then they can give me few cows to lift me up so that I also have a good living standard.

'Now there's this money business. People are demanding thousands and thousands. Before it was just cows, goats, chicken. Because people had them, it wasn't actually a very serious thing to fork them out.'

Life in Johannesburg

'We got a house in Dobsonville in 1958 near Roodepoort, 20 kilometers from Johannesburg. It was easy to get the house because my husband was working at the mines. The mine houses for married couples were full so the mine got us the house.

'In 1959 my husband became a dressmaker. He had a little shop in Sophiatown — the time when Sophiatown was still there! He took me to knitting school to learn to use the knitting machine and he bought me a knitting machine. In the shop he sewed and I knitted. In 1961 we separated, we did not get on. I went to stay with my parents in Alexandra.

'My parents had moved from the farms because my brother had a little business in Alexandra. He took my parents to come and assist in looking after his children. My brother had nine children. After I went back to my parents I got a job in Edenvale Hospital, as an assistant nurse. I worked there for four years.

'In 1964 my husband came for me and we reconciled. At that time I had a room in Alexandra. In 1966 I had a third child and we moved from Alexandra and went to Pietersburg and stayed there until 1973, when we divorced. I came back to Johannesburg and I got work. In 1975 I got married to Smile my present husband.'

Joining the union

'In 1974 I was working at Heinemann Electric and was approached by Mawu [Metal and Allied Workers Union]. After they'd explained what trade unions were we became committed and joined up the rest of the factory. There were 606 workers in Heinemann, mostly women.

'In three months we managed to organise almost the entire plant. I was elected the shop steward and was one of the main people pushing the union. I became an excutive member at that time.

'In 1976 we were all dismissed after a strike and management re-instated selectively. In 1977, I started working for Mawu. I was the only woman organiser in Mawu in the Transvaal.

'I worked with these men for about two years and was then nominated to get T & GWU [Transport and General Workers' Union] off the ground in October 1978. There were mostly men in the metal plants where Mawu organised, except at Tensile Rubber where there were a few women, and there were still no other women organisers.'

A woman amongst men

'It was a real problem at the beginning but I learned to live with it. I felt inferior all the time, maybe because we African women are taught to think that we're inferior to men.

'They expected me to do things. For example, at lunch time people would put in money and they'd nominate me to go and buy lunch with the excuse that I could choose better because I'm a woman. It became a habit that every lunch time I ran around buying lunch, making tea for them, after that washing the dishes. My job would fall behind because I'd have to finish all the jobs they left behind from lunch time.

Lesley Lawson

'Some of the young guys had already realised this was no good and suggested we should start rotating buying lunch. It was the young ones not the old ones.

'By the end I was quite happy because other organisers were prepared to share the jobs with me. I got used to resisting, saying "I'm not here to become tea girl". But at first it was hard.'

A union wife

'After I became a shop steward we had many meetings, maybe twice a week. Our management was very hard so we needed to plan a lot. We'd have these meetings after work.

'My husband expects me to be home between 5.30 and 6.00pm. Sometimes I wouldn't go home because we'd have meetings at our centre in Tembisa and I was living in Alexandra.

'Sometimes it was too late to go home and I'd sleep with

friends. That made him very unhappy and it made our life very miserable. He couldn't see why I was involved in this. He was scared that I'd be in politics and land in jail. He thought I was making excuses about meetings when I was going out.

'When we got dismissed it was worse because he felt I deserved it. How could we overpower the management? I encouraged him to organise at his place. He was a worker at the laboratory in Jeppe and they had no union.

'My husband said I had no time for him anymore. Often we would have day long meetings on weekends in Alexandra. You know what husbands are like. He'd complain that I don't cook, make tea or do washing for him. It's true that I preferred to do the washing at night rather than miss any meeting. But he wasn't too happy and said that wasn't the answer. He needed me to be with him. But he couldn't put me off because I felt it was important to carry on. Now he's got used to it and he doesn't worry so much. He's getting old.

'That's the problem with married women in the organisation. You're in the middle and don't know what to do. If you think of the problems at home you don't concentrate at work and get depressed. What attitude will you get from your husband and even your children?

'One of our organisers had to break his marriage. His wife couldn't stand it. She felt she wasn't useful to him. She was young and didn't understand. Maybe because she wasn't a worker before. But even if she was she didn't think it was worthwhile for her husband to stay away. She was not committed.

'My husband didn't take anything in the union into account. It was as though I'd gone for my own purposes. He didn't think he could assist.

'Our people think the work in the house is the woman's job. In town there isn't anything for the men to do like there is on the farm. The men come from work, take the paper, sit on the chair and relax. Even if the man arrives home earlier he'll never make you a cup of tea. It's in his mind that I must do all this because I'm a woman.

'So you have to have a job, be in the union and run the home all at the same time. If you're a young woman maybe there's also a baby to look after. In the mornings you take your child to a creche or an old woman. If the man comes earlier he hasn't the ability to go and fetch the child and look after it while she's still working. He expects the woman to go and fetch the baby, put it behind her back, get to the stove and cook for him ... and he's busy reading the paper.

'And we do it happily because we grew up that way, we saw our parents do it and we think it's the African law.'

Lesley Lawson

Women's problems at work

'Most T & G members are men. But at present we're organising women cleaners in Anglo-American who work day and night shift.

'They have tremendous problems, especially the night shift. They leave Soweto at about 5pm but they cook so the husbands find food ready when they return home. They also clean the house. They finish work at 3am and have to wait until it's clear to catch the train. When they get home their husbands are usually gone already. They leave a mess, the bed unmade. He can't do anything, not even wash the dishes. So she cleans again ... it's routine. This poor woman has no chance, at home or at work. Some only get half of Saturday and Sunday at home.

'If they start work at 6pm they have a terrible time with the indunas [literally chiefs, but here meaning supervisors]. Most of them complain about "love abuse", because it's in the middle of the night. If she resists or argues then she knows she's in bad books, and can be reported as lazy and kicked out. They also have to work very hard. The tenants seem to make no effort to keep the offices tidy.

'The most terrible thing is that Anglo-American isn't intending to promote women as supervisors. They haven't yet had a woman supervisor. There must always be a man to chase after you. Even the capitalists think men are superior. The women want to know why a woman with ten to 15 years doesn't get promoted whilst a man can come with two to three years and get promotion to supervisor.'

Women joining the union

'At Heinemann we had six women shop stewards out of 12. This was because we insisted and our organiser, Khubeka, encouraged us. But our chairman was a man.

'During meetings we tried to fight the undermining of women's suggestions. They thought we were not saying strategic things. But we managed to fight that. If a woman stands up and puts a motion or a suggestion it should be taken into consideration.

'We succeeded in Heinemann because women outnumbered men. Women took the lead when we were on strike. They weren't scared even when the police were trying to thrash us and scare us with dogs. I think that's when the women realised that women too can be determined.

'We now have some shop stewards from Anglo and even though they're not taking the lead, they're actually participating quite well. It may be because these men have been organised by me that they give them respect.

'No union has yet elected a branch chairlady. Offhand, I don't know even of a chairlady of the shop-stewards committee. Perhaps a female treasurer, since people think a woman is more responsible and will be more careful with the money.'

Improving the situation for women

'The women officials should have their own grouping to discuss the day-to-day problems that we encounter in the union. Having meetings of women is the first step. We can't just discuss it generally. Maybe lectures later as an educational thing which will be transferred to our male executives and general membership. We must understand how we should work as a team. Not have that spirit of undermining a person because she's a woman.

'If we could give an education particularly to the young ones, it would not only assist the organisation but even their families. This business of oppressing women at home with unnecessary jobs would perhaps come to an end and they will help out.

'We pay subs equally, we work the same shifts, we work the same jobs, we participate in the same way in the unions. I don't see why we can't have an equal say and equal rights! Why can't we have a right to have a say in one grouping, even if at home we are suffering?

'I think it's the time for women to come together and see this thing as a major problem for us. Eventually we must achieve the same rights. And we must think of many ways of doing it. It's a problem that will go ahead from one generation to another if we don't actually work on it. I wouldn't like my child to grow up the same way I did. I would like my grandchildren to actually feel free, in organisations, at home, everywhere.

'The problem is that we women accepted it. We didn't fight it from the beginning. We felt it was important for a woman to be what she is. And so it became a habit and even in ourselves we sometimes become very shy. Say when my husband has visitors and I don't ask him to help me, because I think his friends will think he's a fool. But if we can start discussing these things everytime, our children will adopt another system.

'In Fosatu we tried to have a woman's group. But our male members felt very threatened. The women were happy but very reluctant to speak out. They were shy to express themselves. At the moment were are trying to put more women in the shop steward group to gain experience.

'But the men are still taking the lead. It will take a few years for women to move towards proper leadership in the unions. I'm not very familiar with the community struggle but from the few meetings that I've attended, I see that men take the lead unless women's organisations are put on the programme. But otherwise you find that the whole structure has been made by men, everywhere, even in the UDF.

'These men feel threatened when we push to be equal.'

Paul Weinberg

National Automobile and Allied Workers Union celebrate May Day 1983.

Show The Bosses We Are Equal

The trade union — the organisation through which workers state their demands, fight for basic rights, fight to improve wages and working conditions. The trade union — historically mainly the preserve of male workers.

But times change and women's voices are being heard in trade unions. The number of women in South Africa who are organised in trade unions is still small.

The issues which affect women workers specifically are not yet fully part of trade union programmes. For African women involved in trade union organisation the task is most difficult. African women usually work in the most insecure jobs. They must also fight against a cultural tradition which often does not recognise their right to participate in any form of organisation outside of the home.

The women interviewed at Knitmore, the clothing factory mentioned earlier, felt that they had no option but to accept low wages and tough working conditions. Without an effective trade union, resistance to the conditions was often individual, for example refusing to do certain work, resignation, pilfering, and absenteeism. The management of Knitmore attempted to control these forms of 'informal resistance'. They conducted body searches, exercised control over going to the toilet and through a disciplinary code.

One of the floor managers said, 'Stealing is a sore point. There is hardly any in my section now, but it took years to get rid of. At one stage even yarn was disappearing. They were all caught in the end.

'It's just unreal what they did at times. It was mainly women. I had cases where women would put socks under their sanitary towels. We never used to check there until one day the searcher made them check. And they were caught out. I have now even stopped them taking the waste.'

It is hard to believe that the company lost so much money through pilfering that they had to strip women's sanitary towels. Management probably wanted to teach workers the idea of 'property ownership' and to remind them that they were there only to work.

A middle manager commented on toilet controls, 'Women sneak from the job. I used to have a constant flow to the toilet, so I had it locked and they had to ask for the key. But it didn't work, as the last one to go would leave it open. And then they stole the lock. Then we tried a signing system. We tried so many things. Then I warned them that money would be taken off. The business only finally finished when a few were fired.'

Tension

Male workers in the machine section described incidents where violence had erupted either against managerial staff, or between workers. These incidents were often because workers were afraid of being retrenched. Tensions between women workers did not erupt in such violence, but were often related to pressures of production.

One woman said, 'The women often argue about sharing work. If one is finding her work very heavy and needs assistance often others are reluctant to help.' Her manager blamed these tensions on the fact that workers were women, rather than on their experience of work.

He said, 'Women are all the same, really. Black, and white...often arguing about little things. Sometimes they then become big things. But then the women have never broken a machine like the men do when they are angry. Women don't do this sort of thing. With the men — if you catch them out they want to hit back, and if they can't use the fist then they break the machine.'

The way in which women cope by arguing with one another is not the inevitable response of women because they are

Lesley Lawson

Bodysearch — teaching workers the meaning of property ownership.

women. Often women have had little or no experience of collective organisation and action in other aspects of their lives. So when faced with problems at work they sometimes respond in an individualistic way. Trade unions organising women obviously have to take this fact into account, and trade union organisers spend many hours dealing with individual problems before the possibility of collective organisation is realised.

The workers at Knitmore were all members of the National Union of Clothing Workers (NUCW), according to a closed shop agreement. The union has an exclusively African membership (22 000 in 1983). It was established as a 'parallel' union to the Garment Workers Union (with white, coloured and Indian membership) at a time when African trade unions were not recognised in legislation.

At this time they were excluded from all official state bargaining and disputes mechanisms. For example, they were barred from formal representation on Industrial Councils (a system of industry-wide bargaining).

The National Union of Clothing Workers operated for many years as the 'understudy' or baby sister of the Garment Workers Union. Since 1979 when the Labour Relations Act was amended, the system has gone 'non-racial.' All unions irrespective of the race of their membership, are recognised in law. So the NUCW is now officially able to stand on its own. But it is still conservative.

Lucy Mvubelo, the general secretary of the union, said in 1974, 'An organised labour force is more beneficial to both the employer and the employee. The female worker is disciplined and has the full knowledge that she is part of the establishment and thus contributes to better productivity and less absenteeism. She feels the responsibility she has to play in the establishment.'[1]

In 1980 she said, 'If the production drops then the employer always phones us and says "come and talk to your people. — I don't know what is happening," and so on. We speak to the workers and try and tell them that we won't be able to get more money for you at the next negotiations because you people don't want to produce.'[2]

Although they were members of the union through the provision of the closed shop, Knitmore workers were not impressed with what it had to offer. One of the shop stewards in the factory said, 'It is a disappointing union. There is nothing they can do to help the workers. They never come to address the workers. Only when there is something important to tell the people, like when there is going to be an increment or additional deductions. That is usually about twice a year.'

The shop stewards did not feel that they should be involved in the process of bargaining for wages.

Another worker commented on the absence of shop stewards in the clothing section of Knitmore, 'They say they are scared of being fired for being a shop steward. That is why I am scared. I am lazy to talk up. It's too bad. What if you are fired? One person said a union should threaten the employers not to fire you. But the union just says they will come if you are fired and they will find you another job. But in this case it means you are working from factory to factory. You must find something to threaten the employers.'

Many of the workers interviewed had in fact never heard of the union. 'We just go to Miss Lizzie with our problems. I never saw the union.'

The union is important. Not because it has made any major advances for workers in the clothing industry. It is important because it dominates the industry and excludes other more progressive unions.

It is difficult to woo membership from an established union with a closed shop agreement. The independent progressive unions have only recently begun to make inroads into the garment industry. Since women are concentrated in large numbers in this industry, this has had a very serious effect on the extent of the organisation of women workers in general.

In both the textile industry (where women workers are also concentrated in relatively large numbers) and the garment industry, there are a number of other conservative, management-oriented unions.

Independent trade unions and women

Independent trade union organisation is growing rapidly. But the independent unions have not yet successfully reached women workers in industries in which women are concentrated.

The National Union of Textile Workers (NUTW), an affiliate of the Federation of SA Trade Unions (Fosatu) is one notable exception. The union organises nationally and in 1983 had 18 000 members. Its largest base is in the textile industry in Natal.

Since its establishment in 1973, the union has had a long, bitter battle with textile bosses. In particular the union has clashed with the notorious Frame Group which dominates the textile industry in South Africa. NUTW has fought a ten year battle with this group for union recognition.

There are of course, other independent trade unions with fairly large female membership. The Food and Canning Workers Union, and the Sweet Food and Allied Workers Union (a Fosatu affiliate), are two.

Women are becoming more active in the independent trade union movement, but they are still largely absent from the leadership.

Lydia Kompe of the Transport and General Workers Union, a Fosatu affiliate, speaking at an open lecture in July 1983 said, 'Women have shown commitment in the trade unions. They have shown bravery. They have been active in the shop stewards' committees. We have got unions where the majority of members are women. But why have we not seen a woman as chairperson of one of these unions? And where are the women presidents? And I don't expect the answer: It's because they are women.'[3]

Lydia Kompe explained why women do not take leadership positions, 'The women start to feel the pressures at home. Not only is it dangerous for a woman to attend meetings late at night, but she also knows that when she gets home she will find everything as she left it. Her husband will be sitting idle. And he might not believe she's been in a meeting — he will accuse her of going around.

'This makes her retreat. She doesn't want to lose her family for the union, even if she's committed to it. So the organisation becomes weakened. The people who weaken it are those who say they are committed but don't see the need to assist in the liberation of women.'[4]

At the same meeting Maggie Magubane, at the time General Secretary of the Sweet Food and Allied Workers Union (SFAWU) said, 'Old practices die hard. However with discussion around democracy and equality within the unions, and the increasing involvement of women in trade unions, we hope to start changing attitudes.

'But it is not enough to simply discuss these things. We have to act...we must educate our membership. Maybe we even need a women's caucus as a forum within the trade union movement — a forum where women can gain more confidence. We must not be scared. Trade unions in other countries have dealt constructively with these problems.'[5]

Maggie Magubane talked of the efforts of the SFAWU. The union uses wage negotiations to demand equal wages between men and women. Legislation only makes provision for equal minimum wages. Above the minimum, employers can pay discriminatory wages. Maternity leave has also been a focus of attention, as have health and safety issues, to a lesser extent.

Maggie said, 'We need to act now for we don't want to wake up in years to come and find that women have been behind in the struggle. We need to break down every division between men and women, by taking on the problems face to face. One thing is for sure, if we don't address the problems the bosses will play the women off against the men.'

'... with discussion around democracy and equality within the unions, and the increasing involvement of women ... we hope to start changing attitudes.'

Some of the men in the audience were not convinced. An organiser said, 'I can agree with women's liberation. But I cannot accept that women are exploited at home. At work, yes. I do believe this — that we don't expect the women to pull the oxen at the front. We expect to work for our women. We expect to be soldiers!

'While I agree we have got women organising in our struggle I'm not sure that we should put them in the frontline or if they should look after the casualties at the back. When you are in the army, you fire and shoot, and you expect if you get hurt there will be someone at the back to look after you.'[6]

This view is shared by many activists both in the trade unions and in political organisations. It is a view which women themselves have to challenge, for as a woman in the audience stated, 'How can we join hands with men when you still regard women as minors? Stop treating us like computers to operate 24 hours a day.'[7]

And a male shop steward said, 'It's high time we surrendered, brothers...This is the struggle, and for the sake of the struggle we should be hand in hand. If we're both in the struggle — my wife and I — and we are both working, then when I get home I must not rest while my wife carries on for 24 hours.

'Women are now doing a double job. We say we are the oppressed nation, but women are more oppressed. They go to work and then start again at home. We should put aside the whisky and make the fire if the wife is not yet home. And also carry the child. After all, it's the man's child also. We must appeal to our bosses. Pregnant women's jobs must be protected. If not, we are oppressing our women. And bosses will see to it that they can pay lower wages to women — and some time they'll chuck us out. Then we will cry! So its high time we showed the bosses we're equal.'[8]

FOOTNOTES:
(1) South African Outlook 110, 26 February 1976, Lucy Mvubelo, Women in Industry
(2) Ibid
(3) South African Labour Bulletin Vol.9, No.3, pg 11
(4) Ibid p11
(5) Ibid p12
(6) Ibid p13
(7) Ibid p13
(8) Ibid p14

Frances Baard[1]

A Mother Will Hold The Knife On The Sharp End

She told workers, 'No matter where you work, unite against low wages.....unite into an unbreakable solidarity and organisation.'[2]

Frances Baard, or Ma Baard as she is known, has been involved in trade unions and women's organisations for over 30 years. She became involved in politics during the 1940s. She helped to organise the Women's League of the African National Congress (ANC) and was involved in many of the mass campaigns of the 1950s.

'Ma' Baard remembers clearly the days of the defiance campaign of 1952, the potato boycott, and the drafting of the Freedom Charter.

A founder member of the Federation of South African Women in 1954, she was one of the women who marched to the Pretoria Union Buildings on 9 August 1956.

A large part of her life's work was in the South African Congress of Trade Unions (Sactu) and the African Food and Canning Workers Union (AFCWU).

In 1963 Ma Baard was banned. In 1964 she was imprisoned for

Ma Baard.

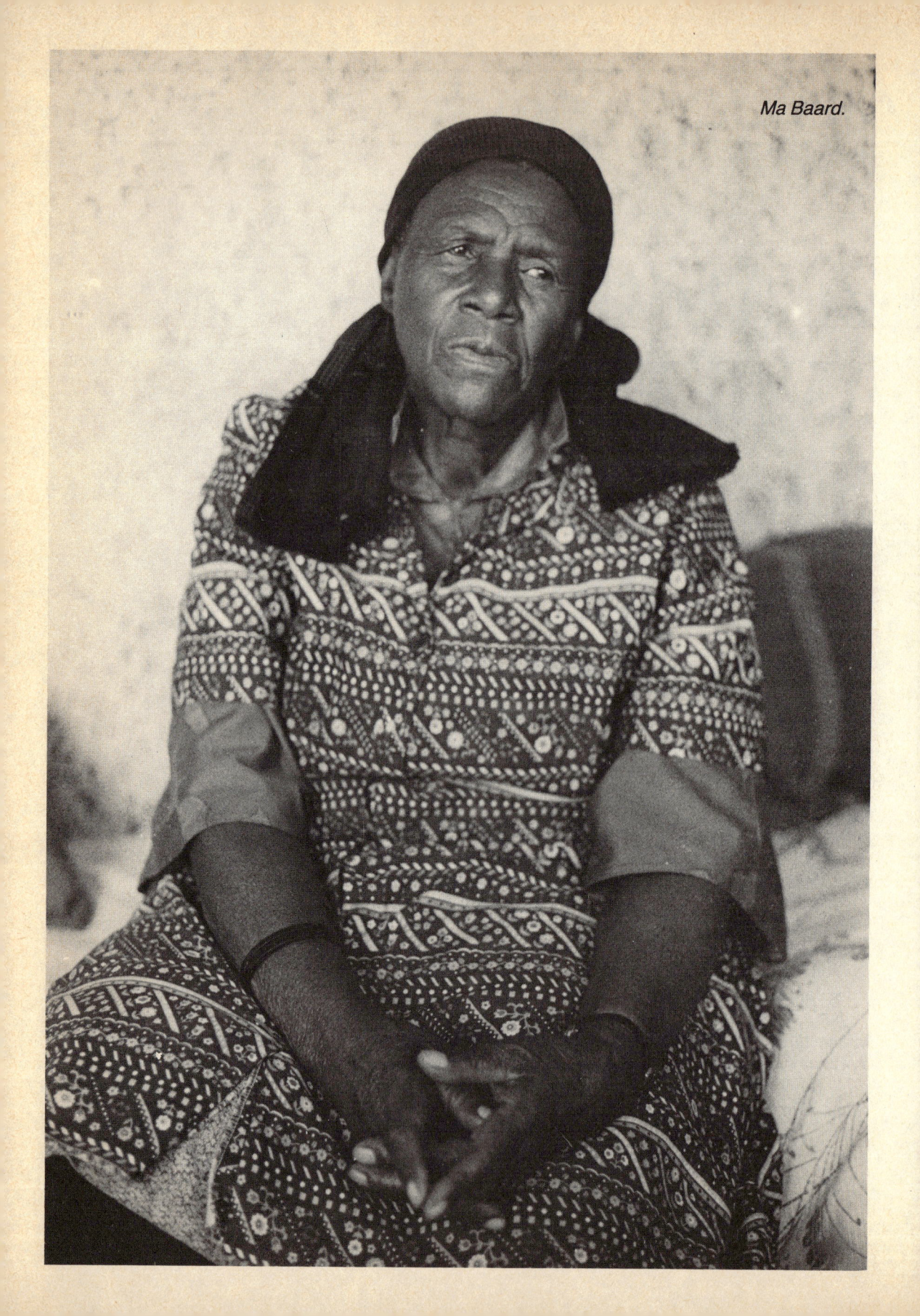

five years. On her release she was banished to Boekenhout near Pretoria. She now lives in Mabopane. This is Ma Baard's story.

'I worked at a canning factory in the Eastern Cape. Ray Alexander came to tell us about trade unions — how to organise workers and settle their grievances.

'The factory employed a lot of girls at that time because they used to get many trucks coming in with apricots and pineapples. These had to be worked to the finish the same day they came in. Nine trucks everyday.

'We worked from 6am to 9pm. Some of us had little kids left at home. When we got off at 9pm, our children would be sleeping and we still had to start cooking.

'Ray taught us about trade unions and we began to be organised. The girls were easily organised because their situation was very tense. There was a lot of work and the girls had a lot of complaints. So when you tell them about trade unions they just followed you at that time.

'Every lunch hour Ray used to come and talk to us and we began to understand what a trade union is. That time I was appointed to organise the girls and some of the men.

'Ray taught us about shop stewards. We went to hire a hall and in that hall I was elected to be an organiser for the Food and Canning Workers Union.

'I left the factory to work in the office. I did what Ray taught me — went to the factories at 12.00 to organise the workers in lunch-time meetings.

'When we got complaints we would wait until the factory was very busy and we would call ourselves together and say that we must tell management we want more money. When it was busy he couldn't say no, he had to give in because if you leave the pineapples and apricots, they rot and are thrown into the sea - the sea was just near us.

'There were two unions in the office, African Food and Canning Workers Union (AFCWU) and Food and Canning Workers Union (FCWU). At the time the government passed the Group Areas Act. We had to be divided in the office, although we worked together in the factory. We organised all the factories falling under food and canning.

'All our factories were organised so our leaders said we should now organise all unorganised workers. This led to Sactu. At a conference held in Johannesburg, a committee was formed to organise unorganised workers. We started organising unorganised factories under Sactu.

'We had to affiliate to Sactu because Sactu had no money. We went to Sactu when there were problems with management we couldn't solve.

'A trade union movement is a thing which our people must really understand. Workers become emotional and STRIKE! They haven't learnt. The result is police and police dogs — because they are not organised, not ready to strike. We try to teach workers in the trade union movement that the strike must be the last resort. You mustn't just come to the factory and say "let's have a strike" — that will make a lot of people killed, because of informers.

'When passes for women were introduced all women were told they were going to carry passes like their children. We have seen our children jump the fences when they see a policeman — are we as women going to jump fences and run away from the police? Because the same thing the men are doing is going to happen to us tomorrow.

'Let's forget for a minute we are women. Let's say we are the mothers. We are mothers — we see what is taking place in this country. A mother will hold the knife on the sharp end. Today we see our people being sent to jail everyday — there's

Ma Baard, 'A trade union is a thing which our people must really understand.'

detentions, the courts are crowded everyday, people in exile, people rotting in jails.

'Now, we as mothers, what must we say? We say to you — we are sick and tired of what is happening. We see our children being sent to jail for nothing. We see people being sent to the borders - they are going to kill people.

'As mothers we endorse what others have been saying. A national convention must be called so that our leaders must come and solve the problem which is confronting our country. We've got people in exile — we tell the government we want those leaders to come home. We have got people who are rotting in the jails — we say we want those people to come home.'

FOOTNOTES:
(1) From collection of papers given at the Nusas conference on Women, 1982.
(2) Grassroots; March 1983, page 5.

Chapter 5

DAY BY DAY

From Crossroads To Khayelitsha

After a raid at Crossroads.

Bee Berman

Bee Berman

The name 'Crossroads' has become an international symbol of defiance. Crossroads, the sprawling squatter camp just outside Cape Town sprang to prominence in 1979 after government attempts to move it were strongly resisted by its population. In the face of this defiance the government retreated and since then has been trying in all kinds of ways to remove Crossroads residents from the area. Government refusal to provide sufficient housing for the Western Cape African population meant that numerous squatter camps sprang up on the edges of the Cape Flats. Living conditions are bad, raids by the authorities an ever present threat. Despite this, places like Nyanga Bush, KTC and Crossroads have continued to grow.

The people resident at KTC, like many at Crossroads, are either victims of the serious housing shortage, or else are people who have come to look for work because they cannot survive in the bantustans. Ever since KTC was established on the windy sand dunes surrounding the Cape Flats its residents have been subject to continual harassment. The government has not yet been able to move Crossroads, but it has made clear its refusal to tolerate any other 'squatters'. And so KTC residents have been subjected to continuous early morning raids. This has meant they cannot even build shacks, but have had to build shelters of plastic. These are dismantled every day at dawn and the plastic buried in the sand to be reconstructed at dusk. Despite appalling living conditions, and continual harassment from the authorities, the spirit of the KTC residents is indomitable. They refuse to move.

Bee Berman

The residents of the Nyanga Bush squatter camp are in exactly the same position as the people of KTC. They too have been hounded to the extent that they are unable to live in permanent structures, and have to take refuge from the icy Cape winter under sheets of plastic. Every time there is a raid they flee into the surrounding bush. But they always return. They have no other option, no other homes.

Khayelitsha is a vast township that is at present being built 35km outside of Cape Town. It is intended to house 300 000 people over a 15 year period. These people are meant to be the present population of the African townships of Langa, Nyanga and Guguletu who are to be moved to Khayelitsha. When announced, this plan aroused mass resistance from the residents of these townships. Despite a chronic housing shortage they had no intention of being resettled en-masse. Khayelitsha is in the middle of the Cape Flats. The houses being provided by the government are very small. There are virtually no facilities at this time, including a severe lack of transport.

Bee Berman

Bee Berman

The people who are moving to Khayelitsha are doing so out of sheer desperation for housing. The governemnt has established a site and service scheme at Khayelitsha which is intended for Crossroads residents who have moved. However many people are reluctant to move there because there is no guarantee that after an initial 18 months period they will be allowed to stay. Khayelitsha has been widely condemned as nothing more than a resettlement camp for all of Cape Town's African population.

Sophie Sigoro

I Get My Pay It's Gone

Sophie Sigoro is a 45 year old African woman who lives in Katlehong, a township on the East Rand. She works at nearby barracks. She has six children.

Sophie was born and lived in Pimville in Soweto as a child. She is now widowed. She has had eight children, one of whom died at 20, and another 11 days after he was born.

'I work in the kitchen at the barracks for R138 a month. Twelve of us prepare food and menus. I started this work four years ago after giving birth to my last child. I did not go back to my old job. I was a spot welder and it was hard work. I lost benefits when I left that job because they did not register us at the pass office. They robbed us. I started this job because of hardship. My eldest son who was a breadwinner was killed. I sold liquor but was not getting enough.

'I am fortunate because I foot it to work. It's nearby. We get over an hour off daily. There are dishwashers and the prisoners clean the floors. I work seven days a week from 7am until 2pm. I even have to work on Christmas day.

'We get four weeks leave though and when I'm sick I send a message. They are satisfied when I bring a doctor's certificate. They usually pay us when we're off sick but there are cases when money is deducted from our salaries. I noticed a deduction in my first salary. I questioned it but there was no explanation given to me.

'I leave my young child with the other children whom I haven't been able to afford to keep at school. He spends most of the day playing. He's fond of pushing wheels. I would like there to be a creche at work.

'Although I get enough food from work, the older children are lazy and they do not feed the young one properly. I often wish I could take him to work with me. My children are irresponsible. They roam in the township during the day when I am at work. I suppose it's because of the lack of supervision. They should eat proper food but they only eat bread. They only eat properly when I'm at home.

'I have thought of sending the young one to a creche. He should go to school later. The older children are missing school. It makes me very unhappy especially when I see other children coming back from school. But there's nothing I can do at the moment to remedy the situation.

'I wish I had the money to send the older children to a boarding school where they would be cared for and where they would get education. I'm not at all happy about leaving the children alone. I wish I could get an old lady to look after them.

'My mother is busy because she is a witchdoctor. The children are alone for about six hours each day. I have not been able to find the right person to look after them. Besides I can't afford it at this stage.

'I get up at 5am and make fire and cook porridge before I leave for work. When I get home I usually do some washing or ironing, then I cook supper. I do all the cooking. I usually go to bed between 10.30 and 11pm.

'If I go to bed earlier I don't sleep but start brooding. On weekends I do cleaning and washing. If I had more spare time I would like to improve myself, go to night school, or do some correspondence. As a child I thought I'd be a nurse but my family was poor.'

Sophie has lived in the same house since 1964. She lives with her eldest daughter, her daughter's boyfriend, their two children, and five other children of her own.

Altogether there are ten people in her household, and expenses are shared. Her eldest daughter earns R124 a month, and the man who stays with her contributes R60 — R100 a month. 'But he is a widower with his own children.'

Sophie has to work. 'My family wouldn't have enough to live on because my brothers and sisters do not help although they are well off. I do prefer to work anyway because it helps me avoid all the township gossip and so on.

'My main complaint is that I earn very little money. That's why children are not at school. I get may pay, it's gone.'

Family Life

My Husband He Just Looks!

Get up at 4.30am. Breakfast quickly done. Run to catch the bus, then the train. Walk ten blocks to work. Work all day. The train, then the bus, home again at 6.30. Fetch the baby from the childminder. Cook the supper. Some washing to do. Iron the schoolshirts. Clean up the mess of the day. To bed — it is 11.30 pm. This is an average day for many African women.

'Keeping a family, a home and a job going leaves most African women exhausted to the point of death.'

Ellen Qomaje attends night-school. She wants to write matric. But when she works overtime she cannot attend classes. She must get home to cook the evening meal for her father and brothers. She spends her weekends 'spring-cleaning'.

'You can't in the week. On Sunday, if I haven't worked on Saturday, then I go to church after lunch. That's only if I've already finished cleaning the house.'

Julia Kunoane arrives home to eight people who live in one room. 'My husband he just look! He is reading the paper while I cook. He says he is tired. I am also tired but I must cook. I am used to it because it is our custom. On the weekends I am not going anywhere, except to church sometimes, because I must wash and clean.'

Shared housework is virtually unheard of. The 'double job' is a hard and often unchallenged reality for most working class women.

Problems in the family

For most women life outside of work is a grind of household responsibility and very often violence and degradation. Many have opted to live as 'singles', and often resent men. Other women feel that they have no choice but to accept the situation.

Maureen Sehlokwa has left her husband after many batterings. Her little finger is bent, and her husband cracked her ribs.

'It was part of my life. My neighbour used to be like that also.

'Keeping a home, a job and a family going, leaves most African women exhausted to the point of death.'

The doctor gave me a paper to inform the police to get him arrested. I thought of the kids and decided just to let it be proof in court if I get divorced. He used to get violent only when he was drunk and then he would get very jealous.'

Doreen Dludlu describes her experience of men, 'My husband left me some years ago for another woman. He was terrible to me. Most of the time he had girlfriends, then he was not sleeping at home. And then he would come back with no money, so he would hit me and things.

'It's alright now that I am on my own, although I am lonely. In fact I am no longer interested in men. I am still tired from my husband. When I look at a man now I feel dizzy. There is nothing I enjoy more than my kids. Their father once fetched them. They love him and always talk about him — when is daddy coming for a visit? But he didn't take them again. He was drinking a lot. Now it is happier without him, but they would like to see him.'

Stella Phitsoane is 32 with two children. She says, 'I am single. The man I have a child with happened to marry someone else. It was in 1968. He doesn't help me to support the child. Now I don't want him to help me because I have a somebody, a boyfriend who helps me. But I won't marry him.'

Rose Rakhomo who is divorced feels the same. She says, 'My husband was too much of a drunkard. This made him violent and he used to beat me up for no apparent reason. I used to have swollen eyes, sustained from beatings. I felt I could not take it any more. So after five years I decided to divorce him.'

Rose now lives with her sister-in-law who is a widow and with her children. 'My ex-husband does support the children. He pays R50 to R60 for the children every month. I collect it every month at the Commissioner's. But I am not prepared to marry again. It creates more problems for me. What if I get another irresponsible husband?'

Lydia Sidise chose more drastic means to deal with her husband who was not fulfilling expectations. Her husband has not worked for the last three years. She says he is choosy when it comes to the sort of work he should do.

'I have been talking to him for the last two years, realising that he was not prepared to be interested in getting a job. I then told him that I was going to report him for failing to maintain his kids.' Her husband is now in jail for failing to maintain his family.

'I've never bothered to get to know his whereabouts. This man was like a burden on my shoulders, leaning on me as though he was a baby. I must wake up every morning to go to work for a lazy person. This made me more mad. My husband was not used to making any efforts.'

Lydia's response to her husband might seem callous. Yet it exposes one of the central, but concealed bases of marriage today - the man is expected to provide economic support. In practice this economic relationship underpinning many marriages is beginning to break down in South Africa's urban townships.

In a survey of working women in the retail and clothing trades, 43% of married women said they received no economic support. This is perhaps because their husbands are unemployed, or live in another town and don't send remittances, or just do not bother to take responsibility for their wives and children.

Many single women have children to support. The fathers have either 'run away' or refuse to help to support the children.

For a single woman with a secure job there is little attraction in the kind of marriage where the husband may be violent or drink up the weekly wage.

Family Life

Paul Weinberg

Many women receive no economic support from their husbands or boyfriends. These men may be unemployed, or live in another town and may not send remittances, or take responsibility for their women and children.

Women are also at a disadvantage under the law in many marriages. In a customary marriage, the husband is regarded as his wife's guardian. He has full control over his wife's property. In a civil marriage, the same applies unless husband and wife make a specific 'ante-nuptial contract' before the marriage. At the same time, the law pushes women into marriage. The right to stay in town, or the right to a larger house in a township, may depend on being married.

Of course, even under the tensions and pressures of township life, many marriages do work with the partners on an equal footing. But the pressures of daily survival and traditional attitudes towards women make this a long, hard, uphill battle for most women.

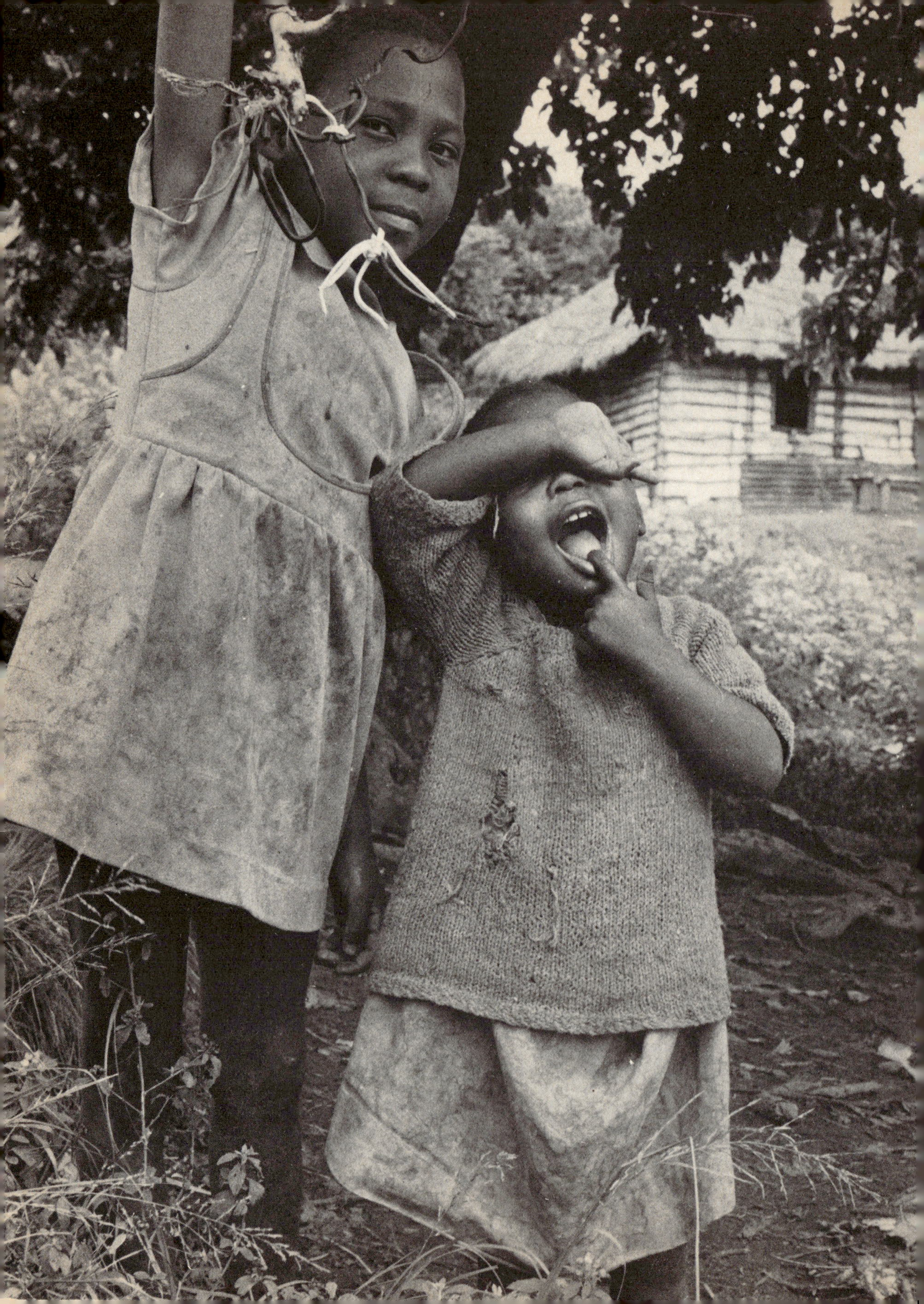

Please Sir Can I Have A Baby

In South African law, childbearing is not a right for working women. A new mother takes maternity leave at her own risk. She has no legal guarantee of getting her job back. With high unemployment she may not find another job at all.

A government commission into labour relations in 1979 (the Wiehahn Commission), recommended that women should be guaranteed the right to return to work after childbirth.

But the government white paper responded, 'Such a provision would result in serious complications for employers, especially for the small employer who has to employ substitute labour when an employee takes maternity leave and who cannot afford to increase his labour complement by re-instating the employee concerned. The Government would nevertheless urge employers to give cases of this nature their utmost sympathetic consideration and where possible to act in the spirit of the recommendation'.

Sympathy is hardly likely to spur the average employer to grant maternity rights. The present law says that pregnant women may not work four weeks before and eight weeks after giving birth. So, they are forced to leave work and become unemployed, with no guarantee of re-employment.

A representative of management in the hotel trade said, 'Having pregnant women toddling around would ruin our image, it is not considered desirable for these women to be in the public eye.'

Another employer said, 'There is no need to make concessions as there is a large working group to choose from.'

Worker comments reflect the desperate situation, 'If you know somebody who is close to management, only then can you get your job back.' Or, 'If someone knows you are pregnant, they will run to the nursing sister and tell her — so that you are fired, and they know someone who can take your place.'

Women who are desperate to keep their jobs will try to prevent pregnancy at all costs. A manager said, 'In a place where I worked before a woman who was pregnant wrapped her stomach tightly so no-one would know she was pregnant because she was afraid of losing her job. This made her abort.'

This man's present company offers pregnant women three month's maternity pay but no guarantee that they can keep their jobs. But they get first preference when vacancies occur.

Many unions are starting to take up this question and a number of comprehensive agreements have been negotiated with management. The main issues which have been taken up around maternity rights are:

- Leave beyond the legislated three month period.
- Such leave to be paid.
- The right to return to work after maternity leave, to the same job or a similar job without a drop in wages.
- Retention of all benefits.
- The right to time off for ante-natal and post-natal checkups.
- The right to time off to care for sick children.
- The right to be given an alternative job should a job become hazardous to the expectant mother or the foetus.

In February 1984 the Commercial Catering and Allied Workers Union signed a pioneering maternity agreement with a retail firm. The agreement provides for 12 months maternity leave. Seven of these months are paid at 33% of the wage. The company also granted 3 days paternity leave and will give R100 of baby goods to employees who give birth.

But employers usually resist the demand for paid maternity leave. If women workers cannot get paid leave, they can use the Unemployment Insurance Fund (UIF) for a maximum of 26

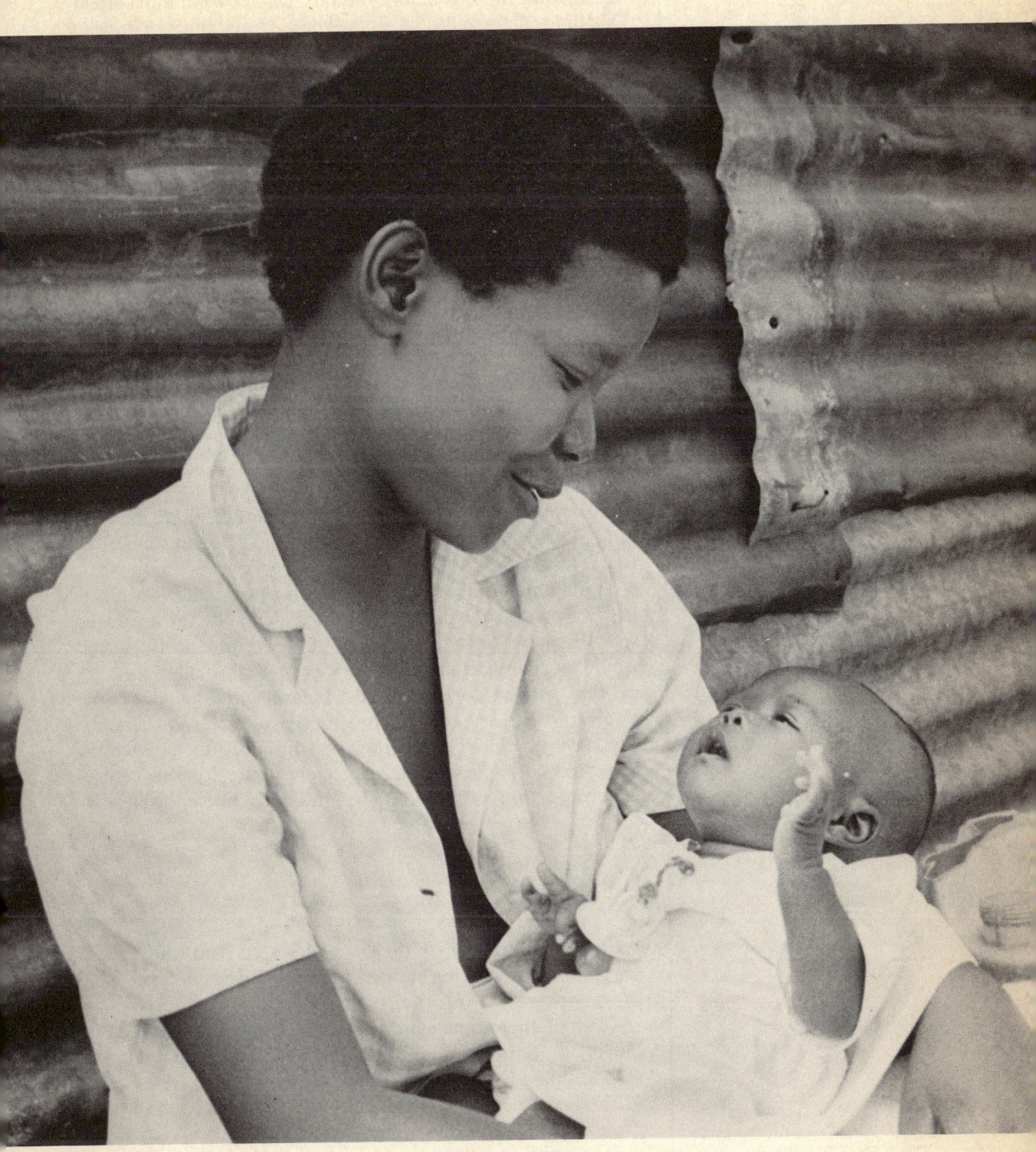

Gill de Vlieg

weeks (four months before the birth, and two months after). This fund offers only 45% of the wage earned prior to drawing on the fund.

Drawing on the UIF for maternity, decreases a worker's claim during times of ordinary unemployment. A worker must have contributed to the fund for a full three years before she can draw the full benefit of payments for 26 weeks. Any break for maternity leave, therefore results in a break of contributions.

Some trade unions have argued that employers should grant women paid maternity leave. The right to UIF benefits, they say, should be kept only for retrenchment or dismissal. Management's standard response is that they do not have to take responsibility for a worker who takes maternity leave. 'It is a women's choice to have a child.'

The government and employers don't take responsibility. This denies women the right to bear children in manageable conditions. Any employed woman who has a child is discriminated against. Her income immediately drops. Future unemployment benefits are jeopardised, and she may not be able to find re-employment.

Also, an inefficient and overbureaucratised system makes it difficult to claim UIF benefits. Workers in the bantustans often find it totally impossible to claim their money.

Trade unions have made demands for paid maternity leave. But they have not made generalised demands for improved social benefits to be provided by the government itself. This would be an important and necessary breakthrough.

Many women workers — those in farm work, and domestics — are at present not eligible for any UIF or maternity benefits. The government accepts limited responsibility for the aged. So it should certainly take more responsibility for the care of children, improved maternity benefits and 'child allowances'.

Child care

Where there are women there are children. And where there are children of working mothers there should be adequate child care.

Most of the women interviewed at the Knitmore factory discussed earlier were mothers. Management felt no responsibility for child care.

The head mechanic of the knitting section of Knitmore put management's position bluntly, 'Absenteeism is higher amongst women than the men... you know funerals, sick children... women with kids have problems... that's why I don't like to employ women with younger kids. The first question I

Maternity and Childcare

always ask before I take a woman, is about children — I don't like pregnant women around.'

Doreen Sithole has four girl children, aged 14, nine, six and four. Her youngest child is too young to go to school and spends the day with her grandmother.

Elizabeth Khumalo boards in an outside room of a house with her husband. The room is too small to take a third and so her three year old child lives with Elizabeth's mother somewhere in Soweto.

Julia Kunene is married with three children. She also cares for her sister's two children. Julia's youngest is five months old and she pays an old woman R16 a week (in 1980) to care for a

A childminder with her charges.

Maternity and Childcare

Child care facilities in the townships are almost non-existent. Women rely on adult relatives and other children to look after young children. Others rely on neighbours or paid child-minders.

child on a full-time basis. She fetches her baby each weekend.

Child care facilities in the townships are almost non-existent. There are over four million pre-school African children in South Africa. Only 0,37% are looked after in creches. No steps have been taken to alleviate the shortage. In fact in 1983 the Department of Co-operation and Development took away the small welfare subsidy offered to black pre-school children. The Department has stated that no creches will be built in the forseeable future.

Women are faced with very limited childcare options. In a national survey in 1983, 885 working women were asked about their childcare arrangements. Half of these women relied on relatives - 40% on adult relatives, particularly grandmothers, and 10% on children in the family. Those who could not make family arrangements depended on neighbours or paid childminders.

The average monthly charge of a childminder in Soweto was R25 per child per month (the average cost of creches between R15 and R18 per month per child). Even relatives are often paid to look after children. Only 21% of the sample had free child care.

Informal facilities in working class communities are much more expensive than creches. But the creche shortage means that women must pay the extra costs.

The crisis in childcare is clear. Seven percent of mothers in the survey left their children alone during the hours they were at work.

The following table illustrates the extent to which African women wage workers use different kinds of child care facilities.

Kinds of child-care facilities

Type of care	Percentage of sample of 885 mothers
Adult relative	40%
Older child	10%
Neighbour	9%
Creche or nursery school	14%
Childminder (somebody you pay to look after your child in their own home)	14%
Servant	6%
Child left alone	7%

A quarter of the women interviewed had at least one child living away from home. Most often these children lived with their grandmothers. They usually lived in a different town or in a rural area. Almost half of the mothers whose children lived elsewhere saw their children less than once a month.

Influx control and the housing shortage in the township are probably the main reasons why children are sent away. One woman interviewed was asked what she would do if she had another child. 'I would send him to the Transkei because we have no place of our own.'

Another problem is maternity leave. Whether a working woman loses her job or gets maternity leave, she will feel great pressure to go back to work to earn money.

A social worker said, 'Most mothers have to go back to work when their children are less than three months old. The children are not breast-fed and can suffer from malnutrition.'

The survey covered the question of childcare facilities provided by employers. None of the companies interviewed provided creches.

But many women feel that such services would not be a solution to the problem. Creches provided by an employer could tie a mother to her job. Dismissal or retrenchment would automatically result in the loss of an important facility. These creches could therefore play a disciplinary role over mothers.

Most workers live long distances from their places of work. Many travel up to one and a half hours each way. So it is necessary to demand government funded pre-school facilities in the townships.

WE STARVE IN RURAL AREAS
Surf Surf Surf Surf
OMO OMO OMO
60c
1.89
1.29
1.19
1.25
85c
45c

If You Don't Pay They Will Knock In The Night

Money never goes far enough. The need to pay for food, housing and transport always hangs like a dark cloud.

Betty Seboteleng, 'You must do everything with the R29 you earn in a week. And the rent is getting high again. You can't do anything because of the rent. When people are making meetings they arrest them. They say it is against the law. Sometimes we get pamphlets at the stations. But I never go to the meetings. I'll be arrested, and then who will look after my children?

'I can't say it will be better in the future. Because in these years I've just seen it get worse. Like the rents — going up every day. And the houses — when it rains, it comes through the roof. But you must still pay R31. The houses are not comfortable. They are too crowded. And the rent — some have to steal although they know they're going to get caught and arrested. You have to take chances. Sometimes you lose, sometimes you win. These people are looking for jobs.'

Norah Dlamini said, 'The biggest problems? There are so many, so what can I say? The lights, the roads, the rent. When we moved into the house there was no plaster on the walls, and

Cost of Living

on top of that they still keep on raising the rent. The new houses have plaster and inside toilets. They are much better than the others. But we still have to pay. If you don't pay, they'll knock in the night and take you to the office. We are all crying. Everybody is crying with the rent.

'There is nothing best in life. The best is just that we are all living. Nowadays you can't live through. When we buy in the shops it's all the same price as it is for whites.'

Dorah Tshabalala, 'The rent is a huge problem. And it is going up again. And the transport is difficult too — the train fare is high and the buses are irregular. Coal is the most expensive item. It is R2.81 a bag and this lasts less than a week in winter.'

Maggie Mkwane, 'My biggest expenses are rent, clothing, food, the dry-cleaners for my husband's clothes and the hire purchase accounts. I would like to have electricity but there isn't enough money to install it. I have to pay 70c a day for the taxi from the station to home. It is too far to walk. The buses take a long time — and sometimes they don't even come. Meanwhile you're standing in a queue in the rain.'

Maureen Sehlokwa, 'The rents have been going up and up. I have been hearing about the protests. I thought that was very nice because people like us even with the education and everything will stay hungry unless we do something. The protest could maybe have worked if we stayed at home, away from work, and gone to protest.'

And Lenah Sibiya said, 'I am affected by starvation and at times I don't have enough money to pay rent. At times I receive some notes of threat from WRAB [West Rand Administration Board - responsible for administering Soweto] saying they will close or lock the house up within seven days as from the date of the notice that is passed. Then I would go to the people I know and ask them to lend me that money and pay it back when my son sends me some money. I cannot afford to dress my daughter who is at school because at times my son has much to attend to and eventually he is left with nothing and that particular month I pull hard.'

Inflation

In October 1984 the rate of inflation was 12,2% and rising. The price of basic foods rose sharply during 1984. Canned foods for example, rose by 14,75% in February 1984.

Many people do not have electricity (and therefore do not have fridges), so canned foods are relied on heavily. Unlike fresh foods and bread, canned foods are not exempt from general sales tax(GST). The basic price of sugar rose twice in 1984, and the price of eggs rose three times. Milk prices also rose by over 10%, and milk powders by as much as 15%.

General sales tax was increased twice in 1984 — from 6% to 7% in February, and then to 10% in July. GST was first introduced at 4% in 1978. GST accounts for 24,7% of government income from taxes, compared to income from company taxes (ie taxes on profits), which amounts to not more than 15% of the government's total tax revenue. Tax paid by the gold mines accounts for only 11% of tax revenue.

It is interesting that while most households survive on poverty incomes, South Africa's executive bosses are amongst the highest paid in the world. Senior executives earn on average R94 000 a year.

Pensions

By February 1983, 614 430 Africans received pensions (excluding the Transkei, Bophutatswana, Venda and the Ciskei). This includes old-age pensions, war pensions, blind pensions, disability grants and maintenance grants. At 1 October 1983, whites received R152 per month, coloured and Indian people R93 per month and Africans R57 per month as R114 paid out every second month.

For many women, pension money is the only money they have. Most pensioners complain that the amount of money they receive is not nearly enough. Although they are pensioners they describe themselves as unemployed. Pensioners are often involved in informal sector activity to earn more money.

Mitta Mgani said, 'I spend my time by getting the pension money. After every two months I get a sum of R100 and some cents. This money is not stable. It fluctuates. So when I receive it I should pay rent, buy food, coal, etc. By the end of the next two months I am broke and have nothing to live on. I have a lot of problems because that money comes after a long time and again I should use all — so what am I left with for survival? It would be better if we were earning every month. Since I have been a pensioner I haven't earned every month. It has been a period of ten years. I starve at times, but what can I do if it is arranged in that fashion?'

Miriam Mosikidi, 'Unemployment brings me problems. Money — as far as this pension fund is concerned, it is not enough for one to live on. When we deduct food, fuel and rent money, you will be left with nothing. We normally get this money after every two months. A sum of R98. It means after six months we get an increase. This month we got R107. When it happens not to cover all I get help from my children and son-in-laws. I feel it would be better if we get the pension every month.'

Liz Abrahams

Release Lies With Us Working People

Liz Abrahams is an organiser in the Food and Canning Workers Union in Paarl and a founder member of the United Women's Organisation in the Western Cape. She addressed the 30th Anniversary meeting of the Federation of South African Women in Rylands in the Cape.

'I am going to speak on a point which makes everyone heartsore. This is the high tax which we have to pay for food. I don't have to go into much detail about the tax to show what it means for us working class people. We pay tax for our own oppression. We pay tax so that our children have fewer privileges.

'We have already heard how much money has to be spent on other things. But when it comes to the worker's future, and the

Liz Abrahams.

Bee Berman

children's education, there is no money.

'TB and undernourishment will spread further because the money we were saving to use to feed our children better and prepare a better future for them must go on taxes.

'Last week I went to the shop and I bought food. A woman in front of me was also buying food. She was old. She had the food in the basket and she was unpacking it. But when the time came to pay, she didn't have enough money. So she struggled to decide "what can I take out....I can't do without this, I can't do without that...what must I take out. I need everything that is in the basket." She had to take out one of the important things she needed to feed her children. Because she could not afford it.

'It is always asked, "Why do the people steal so much?" Because your stomach doesn't understand "there is no money"...your stomach screams when it wants.

'This tax that we are paying goes to pay the huge salaries of the government officials who oppress us, and for the ammo that kills our children. That's what we are paying for.

'How long are we going to tolerate this oppression? Some people say the release will cost us much. But where does release lie? It lies with us working people.

'What can be done about the problem? And there are many good medicines. The medicine is unity. The medicine is standing together! The medicine is building up our organisations! There are worker organisations, unions, church and student organisations. And if our organisations stand together and hold hands, and say we are tired of this oppression, then we will get an answer.

'But it won't be as easy as it sounds. We will have to work for it. There will be sacrifices, but victory will be ours. How can our workers be healthy and happy? Their wages are so low, they must rent lousy houses for a roof over their heads, they have to buy lousy food to make sure the money in their pay packets lasts for the week.

'It is now the time. We must not just talk any more. We must show them we won't stand it any more. And how are we going to do this?

'As the women went to Pretoria and said we are here, we are going to show you we will not take these oppressions. Organisations must come together and this point must be driven further.

'We mustn't wait for the third tax increase. By the time it comes we must be free of all such taxes. No-one must tell us that they will take off part of the tax — it must all go. Or if we must pay taxes, they must be used for a goal for the workers - better facilities, better houses, better education. Medical fees must be changed to give them a price which does not make workers afraid to go to hospital or doctors because they haven't the money.

'What are we going to lose in standing together and fighting? We are going to lose nothing. We will only lose the chains that have been binding us for so many years. We can talk about this tax. But this won't mean it is scrapped. Let us go back and organise, let us all be organisers — organise at home where we work and in our organisations and preach about this tax we cannot afford and how we must stand together. There are many organisations and in them we will organise our people with strength so that they see the point as one person.

'Don't let what has been said here stay behind in this hall. Let it sink in and let each one say we are going to make a plan together to shake this problem from our shoulders.

'Let me tell you a little story. When the riots began in 1976, they were bad in Paarl. There was a little boy....I guess no more than 11 or 12 years old. His mother asked, "What's going on with you." He said, "Yes Ma, if Ma had done earlier what we are doing now, we wouldn't have to be doing it now."

'So friends, don't let us also be those parents at whom fingers can be pointed. Let us organise! Do not let us leave any stone unturned!'

Comparison of basic food prices in 1984

Subsistance	Average cost at three shops in rural Eastern Transvaal.	Cost at chain store in Johannesburg.	Difference
Mealie meal 12,5kg	R7.08	6.35	73c
Nestle Condensed Milk 379g	R1.05	.87	18c
White sugar 12,5kg	R9.52	9.32	20c
2,5kg	2.15	1.87	28c
1kg	.83	.81	02c
Bullbrand meat 300g	R1.60	1.39	21c
Gold Dish Curry 400g	R1.71	1.01	62c

This House Is So Small

For many African people, finding somewhere to live is a constant struggle. In the urban townships most housing is in bad condition and there are just not enough houses for everyone.

People are often forced to live in small back rooms or in badly constructed shacks. Living in overcrowded, unhealthy conditions is a way of life for many people. Workers from the rural areas often have to stay in hostels, and are separated from their families.

Women are faced with particular legal problems. Historically, state housing (apart from hostels) has only been available to families. It has not been available to women unless they are divorced, deserted wives or widows with children.

In the 1950s many houses were built for Africans who had settled in the urban areas. However, in 1968 there were further restrictions on Africans' ability to live in urban areas as families.

In 1968, state family housing was restricted to men who qualified under Section 10(1)(a) and (b) of the Urban Areas Act and whose wives also qualified to be in urban areas. Government spending on family housing was also reduced.

Housing

Local authorities could only build township housing if they could persuade the then Department of Bantu Administration and Development that (1) it was essential, and (2) houses could not be provided in a nearby bantustan. In the same year the 30 year leasehold for urban families was withdrawn.

Township people are often forced to lodge in back-yard rooms and shacks. Some of these are wendy-houses or garden sheds, commonly known as 'ZOZOs', or shacks made out of corrugated iron. Landlords charge very high rents. Nancy Ndlovu, for example, lives with her husband and her two children in a backroom.

'Our present problem is a house. We pay R40 which is the landlord's rent by itself. There is no privacy. We have a bedroom and share a bathroom and kitchen.'

Life in backyard shacks is very insecure, as in most cases such rooms are built illegally. In Katlehong township, near Germiston on the East Rand, over 50 000 people have lost their homes through the demolition of shacks over the past two years.

Sessy Radebe lives with her parents. She has nowhere else to live but sees no way out of her present situation, 'I would love to get my own house. I get so little money I couldn't dream of it. Since I got married we have been on the waiting list. From '76 until presently. My children need a proper family life. Besides that, houses in places like Selection Park [elite area of Soweto] are so expensive that one cannot really afford.'

The overcrowding that people live with easily leads to tensions in the family. Lizzy Zuma's eldest daughter of 22 often walked out on her family and went to live with friends. Lizzy said, 'This house is so small. There is no privacy. There are five people living in this two-roomed house.'

Many women find that being single makes it difficult to get a house for themselves and their families. Stella Zungu, her two children and her brothers' four children live in the two-roomed house her parents rent.

She said, 'I need a bigger house. Here we have no privacy and the furniture is not nicely displayed. I cannot get a four roomed house because I am not married. This is although I am the breadwinner.'

In addition to the difficulties in getting a house to live in, is the fact that township services have not improved and rents have gone up. Increases of even R4 hit the working class very hard.

There has been increasing resistance to rent increases, and in recent years the rent issue has become highly political. The fact that rents are the primary source of income for the hated 'town councils' or Black Local Authorities adds to the explosiveness of any rent increases in most townships.

Katlehong residents protest against threats to demolish their shacks in April 1985.

In order to defuse the rent issue, the government has attempted to introduce a 99-year lease system, whereby people may buy the houses they presently rent. So far only a small percentage of people have responded to this offer.

For most workers, rent is the highest single monthly cost. So rent increases always hit hard. This has been even more so during the period of economic recession and high unemployment. Township rents range from about R25 to R80 per month.

Rents in the Vaal Triangle area are amongst the highest in the country, averaging R40. Hundreds of thousands of people owe

Housing

rental arrears throughout South Africa. In the Vaal area alone, 35 000 people owed outstanding rents before the unrest which began in September 1984. A rent increase imposed by the local town council was the key trigger to the uprising.

Leasehold Sales

In March 1983, the government announced its intention to sell on 99-year leasehold, 500 000 state-owned houses between July 1983 and July 1984. Discounts of 40% would be offered to those purchasing within the period, according to length of residence. Those who did not buy their rented homes were threatened with possible rent increases at the end of the selling period. The government clearly intended to shed itself of the responsibility of collecting rents and maintaining houses.

The home-ownership scheme proved to be very unpopular and by July 1984, 27 510 of the houses had been sold. The buying period was then extended until July 1985.

Not Enough Houses

The official housing shortage for African people in 'white' areas and 'non-independent' homelands is 310 400.[1] In 1982 the government built only 10 171 houses for Africans and only 6 924 in 1983.[2] In Soweto over the past five years the government and the private sector have built no more than 15 000 houses, all of which were for the upper & middle income brackets. In 1984 the government allocated only R8m to spend on building houses for all race groups, compared to R3755m budgeted for the Defence Force.

FOOTNOTES:
(1) Hansard 14 Q col 1170, 9 May 1984.
(2) Hansard 12 Q cols 1032-1035, 27 April 1984.

Maureen Khumalo

No Husbands Or Children Allowed

Maureen Khumalo was born in 1935 in Pietermaritzburg. She has worked as a day-shift cleaner at the Carlton Centre in Johannesburg since 1979. She is employed by Anglo American Property Services. Maureen lives in a women's hostel in Alexandra Township.

'I came to Johannesburg when I was 15 years old. I had lost a number of people in my family, and my mother could not afford to take me further in my education. She was keeping me at home, but she could not afford the things I wanted as a young girl. I began to see that others had better things than me.

'So I decided to "dodge" my mother. I ran to Durban, but she was soon on my track. I made a plan to come up to Johannesburg. In fact I met a man — a grown man who had been a friend of my late father. So I told him my story. He was a truck driver. He gave me a free ride to Johannesburg and there he took me into his home. He lived with his two wives and their children, and they gave me a shelter.

'It took me a long time to find a job, as I looked much younger than my years. My first job was as a domestic in Mayfair. This was in 1950. Here I earned R2 a month living in. In Mayfair R3 was thought to be good. I later got a job in Kensington at R4 a month. I thought this was a big improvement.

'I was still short of money though, so I used to try my hand at selling second hand clothes. Most months I could make more money this way than at the job itself. I had various other jobs as a domestic, until I eventually got a job at Prestige Cleaners — dry cleaning service. At this stage I had to find hostel accommodation, as I was always living in.

'In the meantime I was having kids. My first child was born in 1956. My second child died, and my third child was born in 1964. I also had a number of miscarriages in between.

'When my third child Reg, was born, I lived with his father in a room in Soweto. He paid for my hostel room, so that I could keep proof of legal accommodation in the area. You see, coming from Natal I could not have Section 10 rights. I only had Section (d).

'When my baby was bigger I took him to my mother. My daughter was also with her. We had made up after the birth of my first child — she was like manna from heaven to my mother, after I had run away in my youth.

'The first hostel I lived in was Mzimhlophe in Soweto. This was a terrible hostel, as there was no control over the comings and goings. It was not kept properly. The security was not enough. Men came to visit their girl friends in the rooms all the time.

'That of course is fine. The problem was that — a person could look after herself with her boyfriend, but what if your roommate says she no longer wants her boyfriend, and he assumes he can come to you? That was happening all the time. You could never expect to be safe.

'Now that I live in Alex hostel things are safer. Nobody is allowed to enter unless they have got a special permission. You now have to meet even ordinary visitors outside. There used to be small rooms where you could meet your visitors, but after the "'76 power" this was stopped. They said the visitors could come and plant things.

'These rooms are now used for prayers, and society meetings. Outsiders can come to these meetings, but they have to arrange with the superintendent, who stamps a letter before any meeting can take place.

'There are problems for all of us — especially when it comes to boyfriends. But as I said, the situation in Mzimhlophe was worse.

'I do have a boyfriend and we have to make special

arrangements to meet. He also lives in a hostel in Denver. Sometimes we have to go a hotel. That cost R18.50 per night. The cheaper places are in Soweto, but they are terrible. The place we sometimes go to is in Johannesburg. It's just a room that you get — nothing much, but at least it is clean.

'I expect him to pay for us. This to me is proof that he is serious. It means he has to save. Some women in the hostels will meet their boyfriends in cars. But I won't. I will never be taken for a ride, no matter how big the car is. There is no dignity in that. My boyfriend and I sometimes go to his aunt to meet but it is quite far, so we can only go on weekends, and that is when I must do all my washing and so on, so I prefer not going there.

'I live in a room with three other women. They are very gentle, but the problem is things are vanishing. This creates suspicion between us. A person from outside wouldn't have the guts to do such a thing so it becomes obvious to point fingers.
'There are a couple of kitchens on each floor of the hostel, each with a lot of primus stoves [paraffin stoves]. And there are nice sinks for washing, and hot water. The bathrooms are also nice. The total number of people in the hostel must be over 2 000, because if there is a funeral collection of 25c per person, then usually about R600 is collected altogether.

'I wouldn't live in a hostel if I had the choice. The younger ones complain much more than me. They would take the first chance to get a job as a domestic. This is usually because of the boyfriend problem.

'The much older women — those who are no longer sexually active — are the ones who are satisfied there. My biggest problem is that I can't even have my children with me for a visit. But I can do nothing about that at all.

'I have never applied for a house. I have always heard of the difficulties in getting a house as a woman, and especially with my qualifications. I still only have Section (d), so there really isn't any point.

'The problem is we have heard a rumour that the hostel is going to be changed into a place where meals are provided. This will mean that the cost goes up from R12 a month to R100 again if the rumour comes true. This will be impossible for me.'

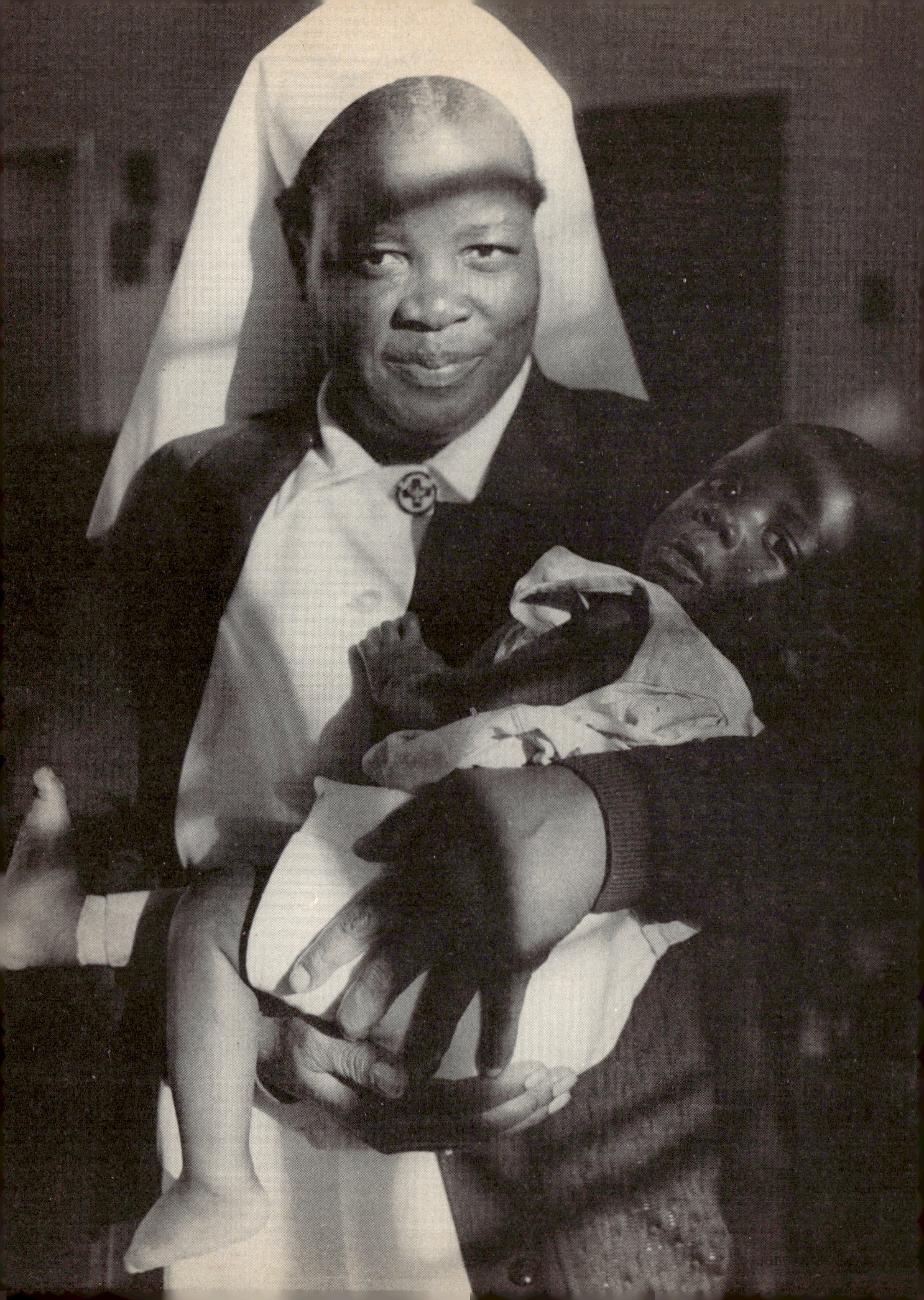

The Colours Of Apartheid

Little money, hard work, no means of subsistence, overwhelming responsibility for children — these things make many African women unhealthy. Their health problems reflect their circumstances directly. Obesity in urban areas is a product of malnutrition, hypertension is a product of obesity and stress.

The World Health Organisation defines health as being: 'A state of physical, mental, and social well-being'.

Being fat

Amanda Kwadi, social worker and activist in the Federation of Transvaal Women said, 'Sometimes black people thought that women should be rounded — round hips and buttocks. If a woman is round it means that her husband is looking after her well, that she has no problems in life. Then she is "Ma Dlamini", the wife of someone who is looking after her well.

'If a woman is thin then she has many problems and her husband is not treating her well. She is suffering. But things are changing. In the urban areas women are going to clinics more because they have high blood pressure, and the doctors tell them not to be fat. They are also being told about nutrition.'

Dora Mthethwa, a domestic worker in Johannesburg said, 'I think they are right at the hospital, to say you must be thin. When you are fat you feel heavy, you don't move easily, and you complain about swollen feet. You get tired of standing. Your feet are heavy to carry your body. Some women are born like that (fat), they can't help it. All the fat people this time of the year, they don't like it hot, they can't even sleep in the night. And men don't like very skinny women. Just like I am now, it's fine.'

Many African women have high blood pressure. This can be caused by obesity. Both reflect stress and tension.

Dora said, 'I first went to the clinic when my periods stopped for five months. Then they found it's because I am taking these preventative tablets [the pill]. Then I had some cramps in my hands. Every morning I found my hands swollen. They told me my blood pressure is high. It is when I eat too much. I mustn't eat too fat things. When I put on more weight it goes up. I knew because they weigh me there at the General Hospital once a month. But it is also when I get a shock. My blood pressure gets high. Like when Joshua had his accident. I mustn't get worried.'

Many women suffer from chronic depression. This throws them into a downward spiral of ill-health. Women eat in response to depression, they become fat, then they get high blood pressure.

But the main cause of obesity is a poor diet. Amanda said, 'In the rural areas people eat food which is cheap and easy to store. The foods people eat are different in different parts of the country.

'In the Transkei they eat mngqusho, which is samp with butter beans. Zulu people eat phutu which is mielie meal boiled in water and made fluffy. But now there is no mielie meal because there's been no ploughing (since the drought). In the Transvaal, Tswana people eat ting, a stiff sour corn porridge. It is eaten with wild spinach, morogo. Sometimes, but not often, it is eaten with meat and vegetables.

'In urban areas they eat mostly porridge or dumplings. It's sometimes a mixture between mielie meal and flour. All these foods are fattening and of inadequate nutritious value when eaten alone. People can't afford better food, and also this food is what we are used to. On a Sunday people eat luxury food: beetroot, pumpkin, cabbage, jelly and custard.'

But fattening as these foods are, obesity is more of an urban phenomenon. In rural areas women are thin and strong, said a doctor at a rural Transvaal hospital, 'It's a mixture of malnutrition and incredibly hard work. The women have other complaints. The endless walks to and from streams to collect water, to and from distant trading stores, leaves many women with neck problems as they carry such heavy loads on their heads.'

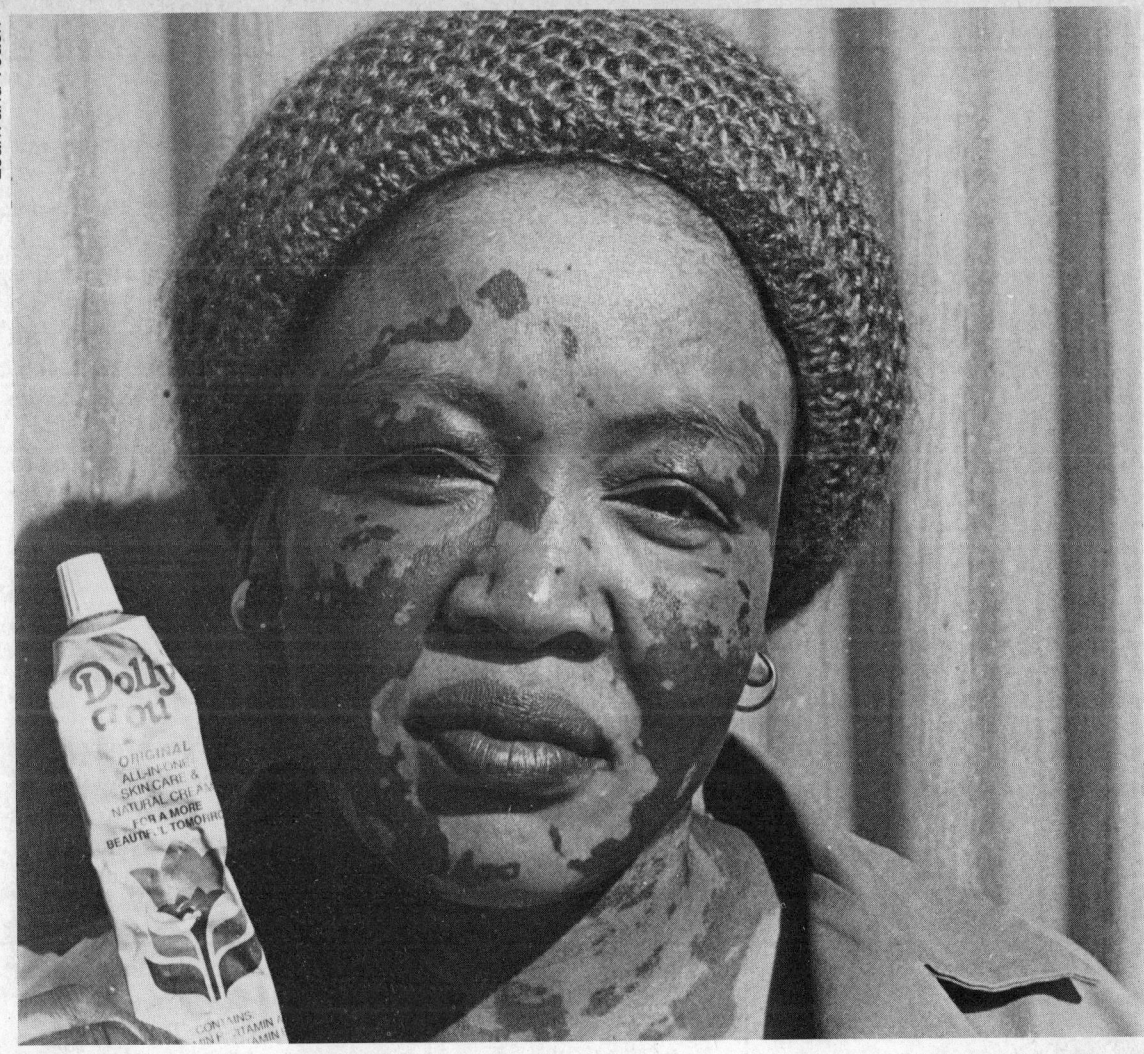

About R30 million a year is spent on skin lightening creams. Chemicals in these creams damage the skin.

Skin lighteners

A sinister reflection of the colours of apartheid is the use of skin lightening creams.

Approximately R30 million a year is spent on skin lightening creams. These creams damage the skin because they contain a chemical called hydroquinone. This chemical poisons the skin. People with hydroquinone poisoning get dark patches on their skin. And they get lots of lumps and blisters which can become itchy and ooze water.

Mabel Khumalo uses skin lightener. 'I use skin lightener

167

because the packet says that it removes blemishes, pimples and dark patches. I want my skin to be clear.'

Amanda said, 'I don't think people should use it. People use it because they want to be white, because to be white is to be beautiful, wealthy and intelligent. On the packet, when it is advertised on radio or TV, and in the newspaper, there is a picture of a very attracive person but it is always a person with a light skin. And it is saying that with light skin goes intelligence, wealth and beauty. If we use it we will be attractive and get married.

'But it does lots of damage to people's skin. Women need to develop confidence in their appearance, in their blackness. The use of skin lightener symbolises the psychological insecurity of many African women.'

Gynaecological problems

Perhaps the worst health problems for African women are gynaecological. At worst women find themselves unable to have children. Until the woman has a child she is not treated as an adult and life without children can be very cruel. Sometimes women are not accepted into their husband's families until they have children.

A doctor at a Soweto clinic said, 'Many cases of sterility, over 80% at Baragwanath Hospital for example, are infection related. Infection can often be the result of venereal diseases, abortion, or the loop [Intra-uterine-device]. The IUD in a woman who has never been pregnant increases the risk of infection to eight times higher than normal.' Yet the loop is a common contraceptive prescribed for Soweto women, including young girls.

Services for infertile women are few and far between. The devastating experience of infertility is not a major concern for the health service planners. In fact South Africa spends proportionately more on population control measures, so called 'family planning', than on any other health service. Infertility fits into the programme to control numbers.

A 1983 report of the President's Council Science Committee on Demographic Trends suggested that population planning should be South Africa's highest national priority. The report said that South Africa will run out of water if the population continues to grow faster. But this is a new form of an old argument. For all over the world it is proven that population growth slows down when people's standard of living improves.

But only when people gain political and economic rights will their standard of living improve.

Whoever Thought Of This Family Planning....

It may be a government mobile clinic in the depths of rural South Africa, or the factory's Occupational Health sister. One way or another, contraceptives are brought to school children, farm women, factory women and especially women with a black skin. Since 1974, the State has been on a family planning drive to reduce the black population growth rate. It is called preventative health, but practice shows the concern is not health, but politics. The view of right wing whites was shown in a statement made at a rally of conservatives at Ellis Park Stadium in Johannesburg. Betsie Verwoerd, widow of a past prime minister, asked whites to have more children to increase the white population. She said seven children or more was a good number for white families.[1]

At clinics, in adverts, even at work Africans are told, 'A small family for a bigger future.' But people say, 'I need children. They will look after me when I am old,' and sometimes, 'We need children for soldiers.' Without adequate pension schemes, children are indeed security for the future. A single mother in Soweto said, 'Some people believe that family planning is the answer because adverts don't show the bad things about family planning. At baby clinics, they don't give a lecture. The

Contraception

government is afraid that if they give a lecture, the people will run away from the family planning clinics and they'd lose their pay.'

But being able to decide when and how many children to have is one of the few things that gives women control over their lives. An old woman said, 'Whoever thought of this family planning, I think was very broad minded. Firstly I think it has minimised the number of abortions. You don't find babies lying around in the dustbins and on doorsteps as was the case before.'

The real barrier is men. Women want to take control of their fertility, to plan their lives according to their needs. This threatens men, for whom children are often symbols of their maleness and virility. Yet, when the baby is born the woman is always responsible.

Women often choose contraceptives which they can hide from their husbands or boyfriends. Examples are the loop or the injection (depo-provera). Women often risk the health dangers of these contraceptives. They feel this is better than having one more mouth to feed, or losing their job. The state is very keen to provide such contraceptives.

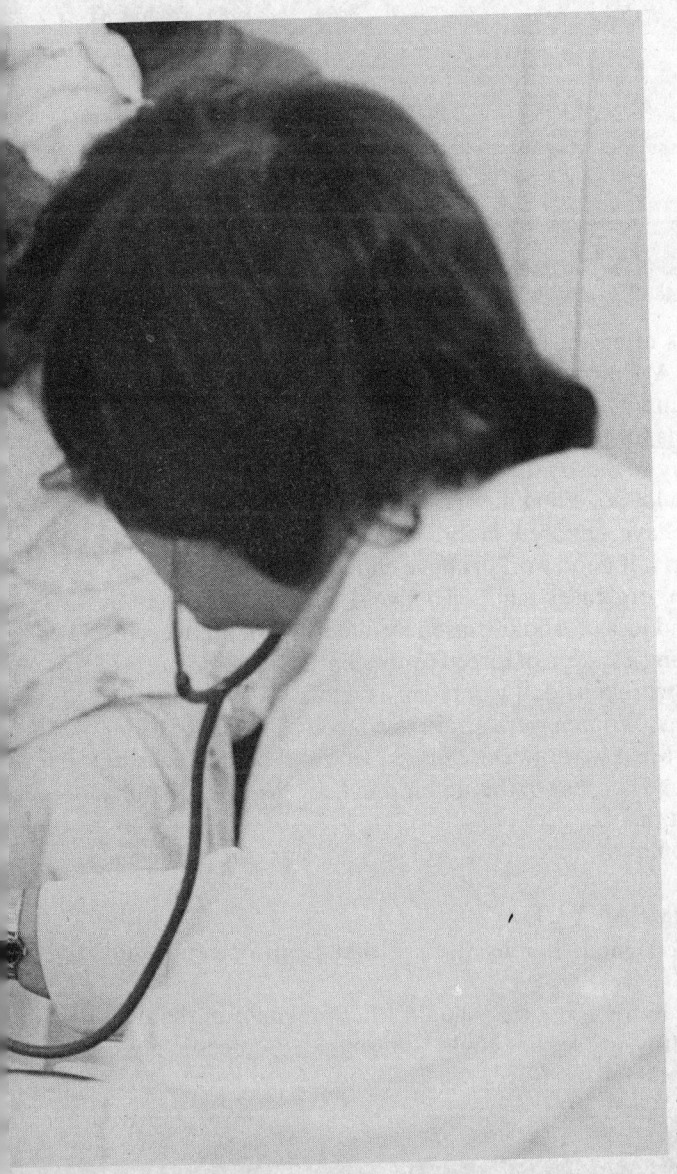

Lesley Lawson

Kinds of Contraceptives used by all 'race' groups April - September 1983

	Pill	Injectables	IUD	TOTAL
Black:				
Numbers	479 892	751 056	40 852	1 271 800
Percentage	38	59	3	100%
Coloured:				
Numbers	165 122	190 741	4 276	360 139
Percentage	45	53	1	100%
Asian:				
Numbers	55 040	11 671	2 041	68 752
Percentage	80	17	3	100%
White:				
Numbers	133 015	32 044	6 848	171 907
Percentage	77	19	4	100%
TOTAL	833 069	985 512	54 017	1 872 598

These figures exclude those women who get their contraceptives from private doctors.[2]

Companies often make sure that their workers don't become pregnant. A Knitmore supervisor said, 'A sister comes from Family Planning about once every two or three months. She gives tablets for prevention. Some get contraceptive injections — not many — mostly the older ones. Some won't go for family planning, a lot do. You know you get a certain tribe who thinks you must have children before you get married. We can't always help it if good workers have children.'

A union organiser said, 'To avoid problems caused by children and loss of labour caused by maternity, employers are now adopting a system of forced contraception in our factories.'

A woman worker said, 'I worked in a factory for two years and nine months. Women were afraid to conceive for fear of losing their jobs. Must we not bear children who will be the pleasure of our old age because of this unfair practice? We need to think twice about this.'

One company forces the workers to sign the following declaration:

..........COMPANY LTD

I, the undersigned, hereby declare that I am currently not pregnant.

I further more agree that should I fall pregnant in the next twelve months, my service could be terminated immediately.

....
SIGNATURE[3]

Contraception

Contraceptives given out by the Department of Health are often powerful and potentially dangerous. The injection has been banned in both England and the USA. State clinics usually will not give out diaphragms. The Department of Health seems to feel that women are too stupid to take control of contraception themselves.

Family planning sisters are well trained in the use of contraception. But with the pressure of their work they often do not use their knowledge to help women.

'In the clinic they are not concerned about your health. The only thing they are concerned about is that you don't get more kids. For example, many don't know about pap smears. I didn't till I went to a gynaecologist. If they cared they would have explained.'[4]

In 1980 the state decided to stop paying for pap smears, a test for cervical cancer. Cervical cancer can be cured if it is found early, but most women come too late to be cured. South Africa has one of the highest rates of cervical cancer in the world at 35 per 100 000 black women.[5]

Being able to decide when and how many children to have is one of the few things that gives women control over their lives.

Women who use contraception often have problems, as one Soweto woman's story shows, 'I've got a four year old baby. When he was two years old I used the pill. I forgot a pill one day, then I became pregnant. Then I commit an abortion. From there I used the injection. Since last November I've never seen a period. Last month I had a check-up. He's instructed me that I will stay another year not having a period. It's just a bad problem for me. The others are menstruating — just not me.'[6]

Abortion is one of South Africa's hidden horrors. In 1981, 200 000 women had 'backstreet' abortions. About 20 000 women die every year as the result of these abortions. About 30 000 women are sterile because of infections from illegal abortions. Whites in South Africa spend about R7 million annually on abortions, both inside and outside this country. In 1978 about eight women came to Baragwanth Hospital each day with problems associated with illegal abortions.[7]

The government will not change its policy. At present, a woman can only have a legal abortion where:
● Abortion is necessary to save the woman's life or physical health.
● Pregnancy will damage the woman's mental health.
● Pregnancy results from rape or incest.
● The foetus will be seriously handicapped.

Even in these cases getting an abortion is often very difficult. The Abortion Act of 1975 states that a woman who has been raped must be questioned by two doctors and a magistrate. In 1981, 381 legal abortions were performed. So many women have illegal abortions. A Soweto woman said, 'If you want an abortion, you ask your bosom friend to take you to somebody she knows. The price depends on the months. One month is R10, two months R20, three months R30, and so on.

'Some go to Bara Hospital with sterility of some sort. But there are some of these backyard abortionists. I know of one woman who is just nobody but she specialises in that. She's very clever that girl. She starts it and then she says, "When you see the signs, run to the hospital." I think that helps a lot of people because when it starts happening they are there — doctors never say its criminal if you come and you need help they help you.'[8]

FOOTNOTES:
(1) Rand Daily Mail, October 12, 1983.
(2) Division of Family Planning in Pretoria Progress Report: Family Planning Programme in 1983.
(3) Women Workers, Published by Fosatu, March 1984, p12.
(4) Critical Health No. 9, May 1983, Women and Health, "Contraception", p69.

Lesley Lawson

Women listen to a health worker at a rural health clinic.

(5) Ibid p71.
(6) Ibid p66.
(7) Critical Health No. 1, "Some Pertinent Facts On Abortion", p59.

(8) Critical Health No. 9, "Contraception", p68.

Chapter 6

BARREN DRY PLACES

Cedric Nunn

Kammaskraal – They Are Dying Here

Kammaskraal is a resettlement camp in a remote area of the Ciskei. It has a population of 1000. The present inhabitants were moved there in May and June 1980. They were given tents, and rations for three days. There is no employment in the area so most people depend on migrant remittances.

Kammaskraal is a place of hunger and despair. All around there are people sitting alone or in small groups, listless and apathetic. Researchers are frequently told, 'We are starving here.'

Most people live on a poor diet of maize, bread, tea and sugar. The people say that they eat meat, eggs, fish and cheese less than once a month.

Two journalists visited Kammaskraal in October 1980. They spoke to adults who had not eaten for three or four days.

'We live on samp because mielie meal is too expensive and we save that for the children. When the food runs out we try and borrow from neighbours.'

Bad health was also due to a lack of proper sanitation and a polluted water supply. Toilets are holes in the ground under a zinc shelter.

One person said, 'There are problems with disposal because most people do not dig another hole when the first hole is full. When it rains, germs from the toilets wash down to the dam. That is why the water is so unhealthy. Cattle also drink from the dam.'

A mobile clinic visits Kammaskraal once a week. The clinic charges 50c per treatment. Most often the treatment is packets of skimmed milk powder. Two community nurses work on the site to teach health education. The nearest hospitals are in Peddie (40km away), or Numpumelelo (50km).

The lack of proper food creates other problems. For example, malnutrition makes it difficult for children to learn. The headmaster of the community's primary school said, 'Children try to work, but because they are under-nourished and hungry, they soon lose interest.' Malnutrition may also make it hard to find employment. In 1980 the mines employed 2 000 people from the nearby Pedi District. But in November 1980 the mine recruiting agency turned down 17 people because they were 'underweight'. Several people said there was much illness in the community because of 'cold and hunger'.

'People are dying like flies, no money, no food, no blankets. The people live in a tent — it's wet, damp and cold. They are dying here.'

We Will Not Move!

'Everybody has died. My man has gone and died, as have my daughters. They took my land away. The Lord has gone — yes — I suppose he has also gone.'

There is a famous photograph which epitomises for many people the suffering of forced removals. It shows a woman carrying a bed, walking away from some demolished houses. With her are children carrying all kinds of household utensils.

Removal is a common experience for many African people in South Africa. Between 1960 and 1980, more than two million people were moved as a result of government policy.

The experience of removal is not only the moment when the bulldozers, the police and the army arrive. It is more the story of years of long struggle, for things which often seem very small.

The fight against removal is a long and bitter war of attrition. And often it is only at the very last moments that force is used. In areas like Driefontein in the Eastern Transvaal, allocation of pensions, workseekers permits and reference books were stopped by local officials. It was only through threatened court action that these were restored to the community.

In Magopa, some months before the forced removal, the bus service into Ventersdorp (the nearest town) was stopped.

Schools and churches in the community were demolished, and the engines for the water pumps removed.

In other areas, the build-up to removal may mean repeated attempts to get the community to agree to removal. The government often tries to find someone in the community who agrees with the removal. He is then set up as a leader and is the only person the authorities deal with, to the exclusion of majority feeling.

Whatever the various forms of 'persuasion' used by the government, the effect is that people live in a situation of insecurity and instability for years.

The stress of this situation is immense. Daily decisions become very difficult. Should one invest time and energy in improvements if they will be destroyed by the removal squad? Should one plant a new season's crops after being told that one is to be removed?

In many cases communities carry on with their daily lives, not allowing themselves to be paralysed by government threats. Often this is the only way their resistance can be shown.

The people of Matiwaneskop in Natal have taken a decision to show their determination not to move by improving their

A government 'fletcraft' in a Pedi resettlement camp. They look good until the first rains — when the cheap wood warps badly.

homes. They have started a spring conservation scheme and are planting young trees. They have also donated some of their surplus maize to the Kwazulu disaster relief scheme.

Often women bear the heaviest burdens of the ongoing hardship. Much of the time, the men are away working in urban areas. Women must cope with the daily problems of living in a community under threat of removal. So they must show strength and courage, and also a capacity to resist attempts to co-opt them. In some cases government officials pressurise women to make the decision to move while their men are away.

At Magopa there were some families who moved to the resettlement area of Pachsdraai long before the forced removals took place. In many cases officials frightened the women into moving even though they had not consulted with their husbands. By the time the men discovered the women had gone it was too late.

The same trick was tried at Botlokwa in the Northern Transvaal. Here a long and bitter struggle against removal culminated in a forced move at gunpoint. But at first government officials arrived and called a meeting during the week when most men were away. But the officials could not persuade the women to move. The women gathered at the meeting place carrying their hoes and picks and spades. Drawing a line in the dust they warned the officials to cross it at their peril. The officials left and did not come back.

The unity and determination of the Botlokwa women in the face of this threat delayed their removal. But often women are not allowed to participate fully in the fights against removal. Often this is a traditional feature of life in rural areas.

Yet communities are beginning to recognise that this can only divide and weaken their struggle. At Mathopestad in the

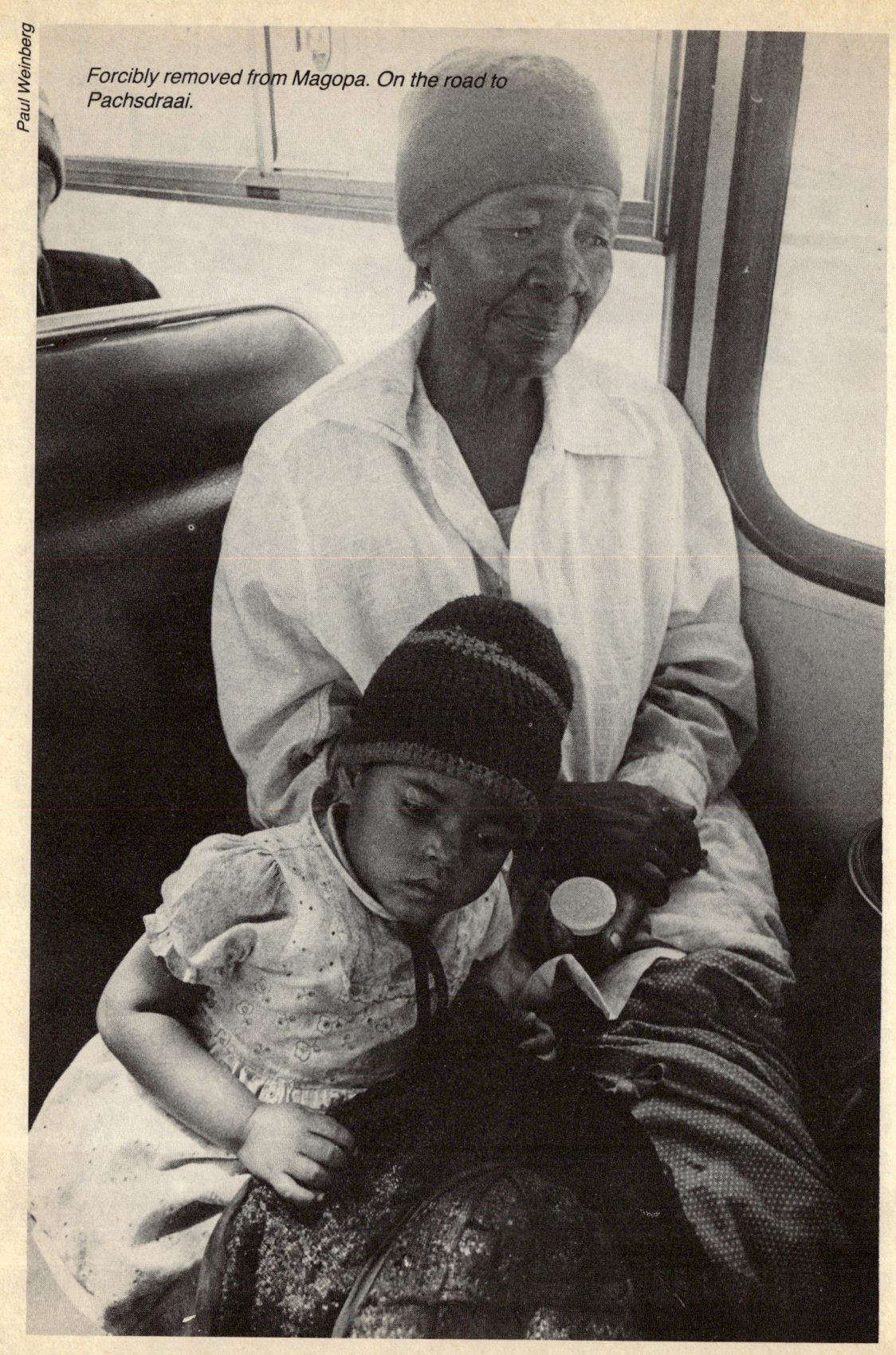

Forcibly removed from Magopa. On the road to Pachsdraai.

Paul Weinberg

Western Transvaal women have never participated in the tribal 'kgotla' - the meeting where all important matters are discussed and decisions made. But recently, recognising that it is the women who face the daily trials of removals, the kgotla was opened to all adults. Since then, there has been much praise for the energy, enthusiasm and hard work of the women involved.

In other areas, women's groups are being established to help draw women into organisation against removal. The Mgwali Women's Group is one such example. The Driefontein Women's Masibemunye Club another.

But many communities are forced to move. Women once again assume the heaviest burden. After removal some people may be loaned government tents for a short time. Others are allocated tiny iron-rooved huts, burning hot in summer and freezing cold in winter. These 'fletcrafts' as they are known, are far too small for any family, let alone possessions.

So women rebuild houses, find building materials, make mud bricks and dung floors. Daily life must go on too, and water must be fetched, wood gathered for fuel and food bought from shops which are often far away. In the few areas where people are allocated arable land, crops must be planted.

While there are many people who survive removal, there are many who do not. The casualties of removal are seldom spoken of. Children die from lack of food and water, from heat and from the diseases which they cannot fight off. Many old people die soon after being uprooted from the homes they have known all their lives. Women have nervous breakdowns, and many turn to drink to escape their problems.

Many women will be removed more than once in their lives. The government policy of betterment divided large parts of all bantustans into separate residential and farming areas.

In this process many thousands of people's houses were pulled down. The houses were rebuilt again in other areas. People lost good land and were given barren patches.

Many people are removed as whole communities. But there is no guarantee that friends and relatives will be near each other. Crime is an additional problem. Women fear robbery or rape. Many women in resettlement areas claim, 'I have no friends, there is no-one to trust'.

Women face physical hardship, extreme loneliness and isolation. In rural slums, women do not automatically open their homes to one another. Crowded together in nameless 'streets' of depressing, similar, makeshift, numbered dwellings, women often feel apathy and take a wait-and-see attitude. Transport costs make visits to other areas difficult. The women become cut off from the world to which they once belonged.

The people of Mgwali are to be moved to Frankfort. All that awaits them are toilets.

Umgwali Likhaya - Mgwali Is A Home

Thandi Dyosi, of the Mgwali women's group said, 'Our organisation is the Mgwali Residents Association women's side. At present I am nothing particular in it, I am just a member. We started in February 1984.

'When we meet as women, we discuss about our rejection of going away from Mgwali, because Mgwali is our home, our place of birth. We want to be united in what we do, because if there is a a gap between us they, our enemies, will find a way to defeat us.

'We have met some difficulties: for instance, the headmen who are against the idea that we have meetings. One headman went ahead to call police so that they may arrest the people in the night, since the headman said we hold meetings during the night.

'We received guests from Crossroads in Cape Town who did some workshops with us. We learnt a lot from the workshops, because they brought us a good number of plans. Through the workshops we have won some people from the camp that said they want to move from Mgwali.

'These meetings that we hold, we call them tea parties. We do not invite people just from a certain part of Mgwali, but from

Removals

the whole of Mgwali. We circulate our meetings from one area to the other. One week we are in one village, the next week we are in the next village. Even people from other villages can come to another village where the meeting is.

'The house in which we hold our meetings becomes full, although we don't know the numbers of the people. The president convenes the meeting, so we know it will be held in So-and-So's house. At the end of each meeting we decide where we are going to hold the next meeting.

'We have devised some flags with words written on them. For example, UMGWALI LIKHAYA — Mgwali is a home; ASOZE SIYE NDAWO - there is nowhere we can go, nowhere we want to move to; NKOSI NDINCEDE — God help us.

'What we usually do when we go to a meeting with Nolizwe is we take our flags and hold them up in front of her, and sing ASIYI NDAWO (we are not going anywhere), UMGWALI LIKHAYA. At these meetings most people side with the people who have these flags.'

FOOTNOTES:
(1) Sash, Vol. 27, No. 2, August 1984, p21.

Mgwali Women's Association.

Eva Mokoena

Magopa Is Our Forefathers' Place

The people of Magopa were forcibly moved by the government to an area near the Botswana border on 13 February 1984. They fled from there to Bethanie, an area nearer to Johannesburg, but in Bophuthatswana. They still see themselves as refugees and insist they will only be happy at their home — Magopa. Eva Mokoena a former resident of Magopa and member of the Magopa Women's Group spoke at the Fedsaw Transvaal Women's Conference in May 1984.

'I'm very glad to be here. Magopa is our fathers' and our forefathers' place. A place that we have heard our forefathers saying cannot be sold or exchanged. We were shocked by the South African government's atrocities to us. As of 28 November 1983, the government forced us to leave the place we have known to be ours.

'We were glad to meet the Black Sash and the ministers who came to help us when we were awaiting all kinds of atrocities that were going to be committed on us. On that day the government did not do anything to harm us because we were with leaders of our community.

'But on 13 February the police surrounded the area. Because we were used to visitors, we were shocked when the police came. We had thought that our visitors had come. At a quarter to five in the morning we saw the police around our area. When we ran to the place we usually go to get help from, we found our leader's house surrounded by police. There was nothing we could say.

'We were also shocked to find that the South African

Paul Weinberg

Rebuilding the road at Magopa before removal.

government can take us out of our motherland without any prior agreement or saying where it is taking us. When we asked, police said it was five years since they told us to leave that place. They said that we were against the government and would be locked in jail.

'I asked one to give me a chance to pray, and he assaulted me, put me into a bus and took me to Pachsdraai, without my belongings or children. When I got there I was alone.

'Pachsdraai is a place of drought, a place far from town, a place of much suffering, a place without water. The water is salty, you can hardly take two gulps. We didn't want to go there. We thank those who helped to take us out of a land of desert. We went to Bethanie because it was a hiding place. We felt it would be more secure. But we are still saying that Magopa is a rich place, more than any other place. We are not settled at Bethanie.'

Graves at Magopa.

Dan Mogale

Donkey Work

Dan Mogale works for the Environmental Development Agency as a water supply fieldworker.

'Most trust land just has one borehole provided by the government. But they don't consult with the people about what design will be easy to use. Sometimes they design one that is for donkeys, so people have to run around pushing a pole, sometimes two or four times. Then a litre or so gushes out. That part of the job is done by the women. If they're pumping water for dipping cattle then a few men who are around may come and help but it is mostly women.

'Some farms have wells which the people have dug themselves. But about 60% won't have good quality water. It's salty. Then some wells are open, or near a pit latrine so the water can get contaminated.

'In one area where we work — Athol in Acornhoek — the people were resettled. They were promised that they would be given land and water supply. No toilets were provided. We had a programme there digging toilets. People helped each other, moving in a group from one toilet to another.

'The government put pressure on the people. It decided to fine people who didn't have toilets. But the government didn't help people with materials or advice for the toilets. And people say that the local officials take the money from fines and spend it on themselves.

'Also in Athol there is a stream. It's always sandy until it rains hard. Then the water runs down. The people dig in the river bed and there is spring water underneath. The last year it dried up. The people were left with the two boreholes built by the government. But the one borehole has salty water. So they have only one left. And the borehole has the same draft power design.'

Omar Badsha

'To get wood we have to climb mountains. To get water we also have to walk a long distance.'

The Men Are Gone

Some women in the bantustans do have access to a little land. A very few can find paid jobs, with bantustan administrations or even factories.

But conditions are harsh for almost all women. Money is short, and it is often uncertain whether more is on the way. There are very few shops and prices are often higher than in town. Distances are long and transport costs very high. The lack of medical and other facilities means that people pay dearly for them.

Housework in rural areas is a never-ending task. 'To get wood, we have to climb mountains. To get water we also have to walk a long distance.'

Most men from the bantustans look for jobs in the cities. Those women left behind get a few letters and hopefully some money.

'My husband comes home after months. When he comes home, he picks quarrels under the suspicion that I am having affairs while he is away. The only solution can be to have him employed near me. We have to do things which should be done by our husbands - communal jobs, bigger home projects.'

Migrant labour '...keeps my husband away from me. I have

to battle with the planning of the farming project. Children miss the discipline of their father. Many families break. Women get involved in misconduct. Many husbands find their women pregnant. Husbands stay away and forget their family responsibilities - children suffer.'

Many men leave never to return. Hostel life is lonely and empty. Work is hard and unsatisfying. Men must seek some kind of support in the cities. The women left behind must take responsibility for children and household.

'Husbands are useless — they don't think of us. When I sue for maintenance his parents fight me. He should return and stay home because it is useless for him to work in cities. He benefits the family with nothing.'

Men are gone. But even so they control local politics and society. It is difficult to learn to make decisions, especially with men in the background, coming home and leaving again.

'My father comes home after long periods. At times we cannot make decisions alone — our plans get frustrated, fields are left unploughed.'

Children are both a gift and a burden. 'A big family is best, but helps us nothing.' The optimists say, 'I would like six children. They will take care of me when old. My husband would like more. Girls and boys are both fine. Girls will get married and we will get lobola. Girls should get children when still young to show that they are productive so that they can get married. Boys will work and care for me when they work. The children will grow and find work and help me out of my poverty.'

But many women now want smaller families. 'Today a smaller family is better — there is no food, no clothing — it's bad. I would like two children, but I have more, I cannot afford. I can struggle to educate them because I don't want them to be like me.'

Overcoming Despair[1]

Women's health in rural areas is tied to living conditions. The situation can only be described as bleak. Medical facilities are not free. The two rand for the clinics means that people don't go to hospital when they are sick.

The hospitals and clinics that do exist are overcrowded and understaffed. The hospitals are far away. People must think carefully before they go. The journey will be long and expensive. Because of this women do not have proper maternity care.

Health workers give lectures about balanced diets, regular examinations and sanitation. But the women cannot change these things without money.

Rural women cannot control their health needs and care. Tribal authorities are male only. They are an elite grouping who often act in their own interests. They decide where to put clinics and dams and other resources which people need to maintain good health.

Thousands of women in rural South Africa are given long term drug therapy as psychiatric out patients.

Ten women psychiatric patients at Groothoek in the Eastern Transvaal, who are receiving drug treatment, have

Collective Work

formed a women's club. They were encouraged by a local social worker. She says that the solution to their mental problems is group work and community organisation.

P said, 'One of our members went with the social worker to another village where the women have had a club for a long time. She was very impressed with the food in the gardens of those women, so she came home and told us we should also start a club and grow food for our children.'

M said, 'I left Groothoek hospital where I spent 2 months. When I came home I just found my children were living with no food at home, just asking some food from my neighbours. So I went to the social worker to ask help with buying food.'

The social worker said, 'When M was admitted to Groothoek, she could take only this small baby with her — it is now about five months.

'The other children were left at home to look after themselves. There was no assistance from the government or anywhere else. That's why these other women had to look after them. They gave them food, money for school, everything. You know, M did not know what was happening to her children while she was in hospital.

'Then she came to see me because she was desperate — there

was no food from the fields, there was no money because she is the breadwinner in the family.

'She told me that she usually goes to work on Schoeman's farm [the former Minister of Agriculture] but since she has been sick, she has been staying at home.

'I wondered what I should do to help this woman. Usually I don't like poor relief — it keeps you alive for today but tomorrow you can starve — so I didn't see that as a solution.

'I suggested to M that she talk to her neighbours since several of them are struggling with similar problems, and see if we could not form a women's group. The group could buy vegetable seeds together in bulk, then work as a group on each others' gardens.

'I saw that as a possible long term solution to some of the difficulties these women were having. They could co-operate and have a joint interest. It would help them to overcome the frustrations and despair which made them be admitted to Groothoek and treated as depressive psychotics.

'At Groothoek they just give them injections, pills and what not. Then when they are a bit calm, they discharge them, send them back to the very home conditions which drove them into this condition in the first place.

'They say people are mad, but it's mostly that they are suffering terrible burdens from living in these barren, dry places with no employment possibilities, no income, no children and so on, that they just can't stand it. As a social worker in the rural areas, almost each and every day you find one or two of these cases at your office. What can you do?'

R said, 'Its good that we have made a club, because we know that if one of us goes to hospital, others will be looking after her children. Five of us have been in hospital.'

'Some of us go every month for injections, others get only tablets. They say we must take those tablets everyday otherwise we'll do funny things', said M.

And P said, 'Together we are growing vegetables and making fences for the gardens from aloe branches because we haven't got money for wire. We will all work together more when our work in the fields is finished. We are still working hard in the fields.'

M explained, 'I've got only this field we are sitting in. It is seven acres but because of lack of money, another rich man ploughs for me, then I give him half of what I grow. He ploughs then I've got to look for my own seed — I just ask seed from anybody who can spare some.

'I did keep seeds from the last harvest, but they became clouded with ants, so they were useless. Then I just asked some mabele sorghum seed from anybody and some mielie seed, and planted them.

'I grind the grain I grow with a stone, then make porridge for my children. Sometimes, I also get morogo [wild spinach] from the field. But since we came to this place, we do not get good harvests. We used to live on the other side, but they said we must move and come to live here. Then, after we moved, my husband died, so I've got nobody who can help me. My children are still at school.

'When we work together we can talk and then the work goes quicker and it is less tiring. Also when you've got problems maybe the others can help you. The trouble is we are all new to this place. We come from different places.

'My home is far away, then I came here with my parents five years ago. They said we must move from our home because they say they are going to make some big farms there. I think that's why I became sick because it is not good to go to a new place.'

FOOTNOTE:
(1) Critical Health No 9, May 1983, 'Organising for Mental Health', p49-55.

Growing Good Vegetables At Overdyk

Life in the bantustans is often lonely and tough for women. In many areas, contrary to popular myths there is little solidarity or support. The harsh struggle for daily survival is often an individual one. So while most women carry heavy burdens, they do not share them.

Despite this bleak picture, there are attempts to break through the isolation of poverty and hard work. Some women are beginning to see that individual problems are also social problems and can be shared. Most importantly, they are learning that through sharing problems and experiences they gain strength and may even find solutions.

The Overdyk Women's Club is an example of such an attempt. Here, in the Northern Transvaal small groups of rural women have formed vegetable growing co-operatives.

The great value of these clubs is that women work together. They look for joint solutions and work as a group. The women's club at Overdyk described their group.[1]

Collectives

'We have been thinking about the struggle we have to get vegetables to eat with the daily porridge . Even when we tried to buy [from white farmers] we came back with empty hands. However, we didn't have the knowledge to grow our own vegetables.

'What really inspired us was a visit we made to our neighbours at Werden. There we saw that the women were growing vegetables for their own families in small gardens at their homesteads. We were keen to know the methods they were using, because their vegetables were so good and healthy. Their fruit trees were bearing so well. They were even selling spinach to neighbours in the other villages.

'We asked how they grew such good vegetables. They told us these were trench gardens. They explained how to make a trench garden. They said they had made their gardens through group work. Even before we visited Werden, the women from Werden had been to a funeral here at Overdyk. They saw empty tins and papers lying all over.

'They asked if they could collect the tins and papers. "What for?" we asked. They replied, "For our trench gardens". So that was how we got interested to visit Werden. After we had visited, we came back home thinking that to make these

'We asked how they grew such good vegetables. They told us these were trench gardens ... Our group spirit is strong, but it is a struggle to be equal, to get everyone to share in the discussions and the work.'

gardens was an easy job. Each woman went to her homestead to dig, but we failed, because we could not do the work as individuals. So our efforts to make gardens did not succeed. Although we were still keen, we did not see a way.

'We feel it is not for the sake of the gardens that we are doing this. Our group spirit is so strong that we will not stop if things do not work the first time. There was an old lady picking up tins the other day. A passerby asked if she was crazy. She said, "No, I know what I am doing".

'Even the whole village has been excited by this project. Many others, even school children, have become involved in making gardens. Even old ladies have been digging trenches. And as a group we are always ready to go and help.

'And as a group we must be equal. One or two members, who did not want to do the hard work, had to be disciplined. It is a struggle to be equal, to get everyone to share in the discussions and the work.'

FOOTNOTE:
(1) Overdyk Women Work Together, Environmental and Development Agency, p 6-19.

How can we solve our problems so that life can be worth living?

We Must Build A Good Car

There are other initiatives similar to the Overdyk women's group. In 1982, women's groups and organisations in the Northern Transvaal met. A delegate, Tshepo Khumbane, spoke about the problems of organising.[1]

'I want to speak about how we can solve our problems so that life can be worth living.

'We must build a car or wagon to transport the community to progress and development. The car or vehicle is built by you through organisation. We must build this vehicle by bringing different parts together neatly and correctly fitted so that its duty may be fulfilled.

'This vehicle must safely go into the community. If this car which is supposed to be completed still has faults, like the engine being a distance from the body, one wheel one way and another one lying on its side, will it ever move?

'No this car will never move. This car which represents your organisation is dismantled by the difficulties you have just raised. "Dikwaikwai" — pride — like the middle class ladies in high heels. Pride in the chairlady or in the committee, who will not let other members in the club raise their views. She would say, "Who is she? Someone like me will not talk such rubbish". This type of woman is here with you in the group, but her attitude hinders the group's progress. She is like a bent bolt that stops the car from moving.

'There it is again, the biting tongue — gossip and untruths - do you think you will ever move? This very important vehicle which has got to be strong enough to climb big stones and to go over broken bottles which cut and hurt before you can reach the community — the tongue has weakened its strength — the car is not powerful enough to go over the hills and dongas. Will you be able?

'Don't you think it is time that we seek for our own God to show us direction? We have been praying for decades but with no solution. Is it not better we look forward for another direction to reach God? We have prayed long enough to an extent of having our knees bruised. We should ask him where our home is and to whom we belong?

'Our children criticise us because when we want to eat, we sell our brothers or sisters for a cup of tea. The children are aware that we are the people who believe in the saying "everyone for himself". We want to eat alone and not share. If there is a piece of food to be grabbed, it stimulates the biting tongue.

'These are the problems which stop us from tackling even the problems which are easy to solve because "I come first". "I have my own car, why should I worry about them? I will go and fetch my own goods or feed". It is important to discuss together to plan and share, but if some are on high heels, others on three-quarters and others barefooted, we will never be able to walk together.'

FOOTNOTES:
(1) Link No 32, 1982, Environmental and Development Agency, p23.

Grace Ledwaba

Growing Tall

Grace Ledwaba is a rural field worker at the Environmental and Development Agency.

'It was at Mamolele village. I put up at Ma [mother] Rosaline Matlakatla. So we were just talking generally, then she asked me how old my child Nomande is. I told her that Nomande is ll. And she asked me why is my daughter taller than her daughter Georgina who is the same age. She said my daughter is taller and more organised because she can wash dishes and she tidies up the place when we've had supper.

'So I asked her, "What do you think the reason is?" She said, "Perhaps her father is tall, she is taking after her father." So I told her that the father is not tall at all. He's just average height. And she looked at me with worried eyes and said, "Then what could be the reason?"

'Then I told her that perhaps it is because the environment where my child grows up is different from hers. My daughter is more privileged than yours because she has breakfast in the morning, of tea with milk and bread with margarine. She also eats lunch and supper.

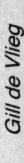

'Meanwhile your daughter goes to school very early in the morning without anything to eat, and only eats in the afternoon when she comes back. So I think that is the reason.

'Then there was another discussion on Nomande's schooling. Georgina asked Nomande what standard she was doing at school. Nomande told her that she was doing standard five. Rosaline asked me if it was true and I said yes. This also gave her a shock. She couldn't believe it that Nomande is in standard five. So she asked why is she in standard five being so young and her daughter is very much behind.

'So I told her that she cannot compare them because they grow up in different environments. My daughter was brought up at a creche. And when she was five, the teacher at the creche took her to start school because she was ready for school. But Georgina only started school when she was seven.

'And where my daughter is growing up, the schools are nearer, the teachers are qualified and the resources, of course, are better. At our school you don't pay for textbooks.

'And then I told her that her daughter is very far from school. She doesn't go to school every day because when it rains she can't cross the rivers. She has to cross two rivers to get to school. And her teachers — most of them are not qualified, they are just drop-outs from her school.

'And, of course, she doesn't have money to buy proper books. My daughter often comes and says, the teacher says if we want to know more we must buy this book. Then I buy it for her and she reads it.'

Tshidi Kompe

We Use Candles To Read

Tshidi Kompe is 23 years old. She goes to school near Marble Hall in the Northern Transvaal.

'There are a total of about 500 pupils in the school — about 300 girls, and 200 boys. In the highest grades there are 34 boys and 24 girls.

'There are 47 girls who board at the school — and no boys. We share two rooms and a hall — 10 girls in each room, and the rest in the hall. The beds are all double bunks.

'We use our classrooms for evening study. There is no electricity, and no heaters in winter. We use candles to read by - half a candle for every two students. We are only allowed visitors for 30 minutes on the weekends. There are no visiting rooms or eating rooms, and so we have to meet our visitors outside under the trees. Every night we have to be asleep not later than 9.30pm. We don't have problems from boy students or the teachers, as our principal is very strict.

'I returned to school in 1983 to improve my education. Before I only had the PTC [primary teachers certificate], which meant I could only earn R120 as a teacher.'

'The principal earns R700 a month, and the vice-principal earns R600. Other qualified teachers earn R300, while the "private" teachers (with matric) earn R110. There are 17 teachers — five women and twelve men. All the teachers have their own rooms on the school premises. Each has only got one room.

'There are two girls who have come specially from the cities to school. But when I was training for PTC there were 95% who came from the cities. That was 1980-81.

'We eat samp mielies with acha from Monday to Saturday. On Sundays we eat porridge and chicken. We never eat vegetables. We have dry brown bread and black tea. There is never any fruit. We use our own plates and mugs.

'For washing we use our own plastic basins. There are no bathrooms, and there is no hot water. We use our primus stoves, and our irons for ironing.

'We are not allowed to go to town even to the nearest shops for shopping. The bakery van comes every afternoon to sell us bread and rolls. We give our teachers money to buy us some things in town.'

Schooling

Amount spent per school child in 1982/83 Financial year.

	R
African child	192.34
Coloured	593.37
Indian	871.87
White	1 385.00

(Survey of Race Relations in South Africa 1983 SAIRR Johannesburg)

Pupil — teacher ratios — 1983

African	42,7:1
Coloured	27,1:1
Indian	23,1:1
White	18,2:1

(Survey of Race Relations in South Africa 1983 SAIRR Johannesburg)

Percentage of underqualified teachers:

African	77%
Coloured	59%
Indian	18%

All white teachers must have at least matric plus a teachers diploma. But some people had put the figure for unqualified white teachers at 3%.

(Survey of Race Relations in South Africa 1983 SAIRR Johannesburg)

Chapter 7

HOLD HANDS TOGETHER

Cedric Nunn

Beauty Mkize serves guests at the commemoration gathering for her late husband Saul Mkize, who was shot by police during protests against removals.

Then The HP Is A Little Bit Less

Pauline Ramugondo describes her weekend, 'Saturdays — the busiest day. I do the washing, the mending of clothes for the children. You know, a woman is always busy at home... It is a double job... You get a rest when you go to church or at the *mtshaolo*.'

A *mtshaolo* is one of the many types of voluntary associations which have emerged to help people cope with the pressures of urban life. Most of these help household savings. The most common are burial societies, and *stokvels*.

The word *stokvel* covers many different organisations. In the early days *stokvels* were occasions every Monday when Doornfontein slumyard shebeen queens (women who run illegal drinking venues either with homemade or bought liquor) sold liquor left over from Sundays at a cheaper rate.

Stokvel has now come to mean an event where drinks (generally alcoholic for mens' *stokvels*, and non alcoholic at women's meetings) are served, and where fund-raising takes place.

Another type of *stokvel* is the *mohodisano*, literally meaning 'We pay each other back'. These are rotating credit associations. The organisations usually have a membership of about 30, each of whom pools a sum of money each week or month. If each member contributes R10 a month, each will receive R300 once every 30 months. In this way savings are kept in circulation in the community.

'Then the H.P. [hire purchase] is a little bit less. After producing money, we then have tea, and maybe some cakes...we make jokes of our problems'. The group meets at a different member's house each time. That person charges for plates of food and drink.

Matshido or *masibanbane* means 'river in flood' and 'hold hands together'. They are groups formed to cope with a specific crisis such as death or unemployment. They are people who rally round to help a member who has suffered a crisis — the support is financial, but is even more importantly moral and social.

Khosi Ntombela said, 'I was a member of an organisation in 1982. It was a *stokvel* where we used to help each other when there was something like a wedding or a death or birthday parties. This was done by helping to cook and serve. All in all the donation was R20 a week from all. We used to meet for 30 minutes every Saturday. I used to go to every meeting. I didn't want to miss it because there was a lot of entertainment, such as drinking wine and the discussions and even dancing.'

Pauline Ramugondo used to belong to an organisation in Soweto called the Housewives League. She left the organisation after three years, 'because I was too tired, there was no time.' There were about 30 women in the organisation, and it focused on social outings.

'I would like to join again. It used to try and give us some ideas for our families. Even if you have got a broken heart, it would unite and connect us together so we were not alone. Sometimes if you had difficulties at home they would put you right.'

Monica Phadi is a member of a co-operative buying society at Meadowlands hostel in Soweto. 'Realising that food was a problem and that we were starving all the time, some of us decided to form a group where we collect R3 each week and buy food in bulk and share it amongst ourselves. This idea helps us a lot because of inflation. We feel at least that it works out cheaper although we buy at the OK Bazaars which is supposed to be not very reasonable on their food prices.'

Funerals are social occasions. In a society where most of daily life is a grind of hard work, it is a time to gather together, to see people and to share experience and emotions.

A death in the family is expensive. Funerals cost at least R800, for a coffin, food for the wake, and the hire of buses. To provide for this very necessary expense there are burial societies.

Kona Mokhoera — Fedtraw organiser and ex-political prisoner — in the street before going to the graveyard for Dora Tamana's tomb unveiling.

Burial societies have memberships of between 50 and 80. Each member contributes about R5 a month until a float of about R2 000 is held. When a death occurs, the bereaved get a grant of about R500. The group then begins to contribute again until the R2 000 float is reached.

Burial societies often contain both men and women, although many are single-sexed.

Jessy Cindi, 'I belong to the burial society. There is one which usually meets on Sunday and one on Saturday. The Saturday one we donate R3 and the Sunday one R5 even if there isn't a burial.

'In the meeting we discuss how to organise a burial and how to fight inflation. In the meeting we collect standby money of R300 that goes to the bereaved. A coffin and buses are paid from the R3 and R5, even groceries. We only hold a serious meeting when there is death.

'I usually go to every meeting. I never stay away because I would like to be up to date with everything concerning the society.'

These voluntary associations place great emphasis on social and moral support. They take low wages and stretch them as far as they will go. Individual experience of exploitation and oppression among their members is discussed. But they do not extend to discussion and action around general community problems or political issues. And the rights of their members as workers or community members are not defended collectively.

Bee Berman

Zionist church women in Crossroads.

They Came To Pray, To Help

Most people in South Africa are Christians — at least in name and most women make time to go to church. There are two main groups of churches: the mainline churches and the African Independent Churches.

The mainline churches

The mainline churches — Catholic, Anglican, Methodist and so on — originate from Europe or North America. These churches include large numbers of ordinary people. But their leadership from bishops to parish councils is mainly middle class and male, and at the top still mainly white.

Their structures and ways of working also maintain class, race and male domination. On the one hand the church proclaims equality of all in the sight of God, and on the other, women, blacks and working class people generally play a secondary role.

Women usually form the bulk of any congregation. Anna Moloi said, 'Men say, "What is the use of going to church, I can pray at home, church is for women. Church is just looking for money. Wife and children should go to church. I feel lazy," they say.'

Lenah Nthuli said, 'Women have many difficulties. We need people to share and be free with. That is why we go to church. We pray together. We share. It is time to talk to friends, to discuss problems. They help you. Women have many problems in the house. We feel for the children. The children need a good example. They need good behaviour. To go to church is good behaviour. They must learn to go to church.'

Women do similar jobs in the church to the ones they do at home. Anna said, 'We tidy, and clean, prepare the altar, do the brasso, wash the priest's clothes and iron them and we arrange the flowers. All women in the church do this.'

But Lenah said, 'At first women were nothing in the church. Now we have a part. The work of women was just to clean, not to share in everything. Lately women are in committees and can read the gospel. Before women could only entertain women visitors, now we can entertain all visitors.'

Women's organisation in the church

All the mainline churches have associated women's organisations. Most women who go to church belong to one of these organisations such as the Anglican Church's Mothers' Union, the Catholic Church's Women of St Anne and in the Congregational Church, the Women's Fellowship.

Anna Moloi said, 'In St Anne's we visit the sick, help the poor and the old. We do the cooking, cleaning and the washing for the old. St Anne helped others. We follow the steps of St Anne. If someone passes on we go there and call the priest. We prepare the place for the priest. We say prayers and help the children.'

And Lenah Nthuli said, 'In St Anne we are friends. We are free. A woman becomes free even when she is shy and just at home. She becomes free to tell her problems. She is shy to tell the priest but she tells the women.'

The Anglican Mothers' Union is typical of these organisations. It operates in most parishes and mainly African women are members. Parish membership ranges from 70 to 300 women.

The aim of the Mothers' Union is to be specially concerned with all that strengthens and preserves marriage and Christian life. 'It tries to promote the conditions in society favourable to stable family life and protection of children.' Mothers' Union members look at the way migrant labour and resettlement affects family life. They then send recommendations to the bishops.

Branches decide on activities. During 1982 activities included prayer groups, bible study groups, visiting the sick, aged and bereaved people, visiting other parishes. Talks were held on topics such as cancer, cooking, sewing, and family planning. Soup kitchens were run, clothes were collected for the poor and street collections for the needy.

Women involved explained the importance of these activities in the community. Doris Motshoene said, 'Prayers really help. For example a woman lost her daughter and she didn't know where to go. We prayed for her. One day her daughter came in. Another woman had problems with her husband. "Remember me in your prayers", she said. Really it helps.'

Gladys Sesibu said, 'The women in the church group collect

Omar Badsha

Zionist church service in Crossroads.

food if you have none and give it to you. They find out your ward number in Baragwanath and go and visit. They don't ask, "Where can we get transport?" They just go. Women care.'

And Thandi Mahlangu, 'Women like to pray together. We want peace. We want everything nice, to be happy to each other and everyone. Everyone needs happiness and freedom, not just Christians but everyone.'

The Independent Churches

A group of people in flowing robes of bright green and white walk along a suburban street on a Sunday morning. The men carry staffs, and the group is singing and chatting as they walk. The people are coming from a church meeting.

The dramatic uniforms of the independent churches set these people apart. Between five and eight million African people belong to independent churches. They call them the 'churches of the people' as opposed to the western 'white' churches.

Independent church religion is based on the bible, and members interpret it according to their daily experience. Their religion and practice is quite different from that of mainline churches. It provides an avenue of spiritual release for its members. This is crucial for their survival in the chaos and degradation of everyday life in South Africa.

The churches are usually made up of small groups of 30 to 50 people. Every group has many ranks and statuses within it - prophets, elders, bishops, deacons, treasurers. Most members have a specific role to play and a recognised place within the group.

This is so different from daily experience. These people are among the poorest in the country. They are humiliated and exploited in their jobs and by apartheid.

The church creates a community of support. Lenah Moloi said, 'Church people are like brothers and sisters. In difficulty they help you and people don't see that you don't have brothers and sisters. They hide the problems so others don't see. They are part of the helping hand.'

Support is especially necessary for older people who grew up in rural areas with a strong sense of community. In the urban areas they face chaotic townships, violence and often a great sense of isolation.

Daisy Mabundu said, 'They helped people. My father-in-law passed on. They came to pray, to help. They baked cakes, made tea, washed dishes and saw that everything is clean. They still visit my mother-in-law.'

The independent churches are structured along very traditional lines. Men take leadership positions like bishop or minister. Women are likely to be prophetesses. This is a position of spontaneous, charismatic leadership, rather than one which is part of the institutional hierarchy. So women do remain subordinate to men. But unlike the mainline churches where there is a division between the clergy and the laity, the structure of independent churches allows women to play a more active role.

The older people make decisions and no particular place is made for the youth. Church members meet as a family.

The lack of youth organisation means that young people whose level of education is often higher than that of their parents often leave the church for mainline churches, or stop going to church altogether.

There are women's groups which meet on Thursdays — the day that most domestic workers have off from work.

The independent churches have been described as 'working class churches which capture the experience of working class people'. African people often reject the kind of baptism of the mainline churches where children are given 'Christian' names. These names, they say, are useful to white bosses because they can pronounce them and so tell the people what to do.

The independent churches give a coherence to people's lives. Although these churches are expressly church oriented, members are encouraged to get involved in political organisation. Leaders are aware that the church may channel the feelings and spiritual needs of its members. But members may be involved in other forms of organisation trying to change society.

Chapter 8

VUKANI MAKHOSIKAZI

WAKE UP WOMEN

The late Dora Tamana — a founder member of the Federation of South African Women in 1954.

She Named Him 'Freedom'

Most women do not take part in political organisation. They have little spare time and often their husbands forbid them to participate.

'There are some leaders who speak at meetings. I have never gone although sometimes my husband goes. I have no time, as they are usually on a Sunday and I must go to church. And then I am busy with the washing. He has a lot more time. I would like to go to the meetings. Sometimes he tells me about them, sometimes he doesn't. There are mostly men who go to the meetings. Some women go, but none of my own friends.'

Another woman said, 'I never go to the mass meetings because I fear police harassment and teargas. If police were not there I would like to go to know about the daily happenings.'

Tshidi Phuthela said, 'My husband said I must not attend political meetings. He said he is scared of the police. My brother-in-law was on Robben Island for 16 years. He was released in 1975 and arrested again in January 1976. He spent 25 months in detention, then he left the country. His wife was a nurse, she followed him with their two children. This was after much harassment. I think they went to Botswana and then to Tanzania'

But these things do not stop women from expressing their opinions. Tshidi Phuthela spoke about Ephraim Tshabalala, the ex 'mayor' of Soweto. 'ET is a sell-out. I think he doesn't even live in Soweto anymore because he is scared. Dr Motlana chairperson of the Soweto Civic Association and the Committee of Ten, they tried. The people want Mandela to be free but the government won't let him. That was a good leader.'

Julia Sone has been waiting for a house for ten years and depends on the good-will of her relatives. She said, 'How can I go to the rent meetings if I haven't got a home? I am not so much interested in the Women's Federation although I heard of it. The trouble is, I don't have time — when I come from work we start to cook and so forth. There is no time to go around. I just read the papers and listen to the radio.'

For many women, politics is something for others, not themselves. Most older women remember the period of mass political action in the 1950s and 1960s, and Nelson Mandela remains for them a symbol of leadership and struggle.

Norah Dlamini said, 'I remember we had the azikhwela bus boycott in Alexandra, and the stayaways. We used to go to the offices in the bottom of town to see Nelson Mandela — you know how it is with a famous person. You just want to know what he looks like. I never met him — I just saw him when we went past. In the 1980 petition all the people were saying he must be released.

'In about 1960 there was a big meeting close to our house. We were called but we did not know what it was. We saw a lot of people — some in green shirts and black skirts. Then we saw what was happening. The people were burning their passes. I was scared so I did not stay. I was living in the shelters in Jabavu.'

In the more immediate past, the collective agony of the 1976 riots has made a mark on even the least political woman. June 1976 is referred to as 'the power days'.

Dora Tshabalala said, 'I did not come to work for a period in 1976 — because it was that unrest. There has been no change. It is not yet right. The children are not happy about it.'

Maureen Sehlokwa, 'My sister named one of her children for the Freedom Charter. She named him "Freedom". He was shot dead in 1976. His brother is now a leader at his school.'

Many women enter the field of politics by force of necessity. In June 1984 the water supply was cut off in the township of Chiawelo in Soweto. In desperation about 50 residents, women included, marched to the local Soweto Council office to protest. They carried placards saying, 'Toilets. Pooh' and 'No Water, but we get high bills'.

No-good leaders

Issues like this can push even the most passive of women into action. Mpho Hlongwane's story is a good example. She has come face to face with the community councils in her struggle for housing. Her story captures the dilemma of many women, brutalised by poverty, whose cries for help are ignored, even by those who pretend to lead their community.

Mpho Hlongwane has spent a total of 12 years in prison, each time for shoplifting. In 1963 her husband deserted her and her two children.

'Times were bad then. What with job reservation at its worst in those days, there were few jobs for women. It was almost impossible to survive as a single parent.

'Bad luck seemed to follow me, even to prison. I had left my house in the care of a distant relative whom I trusted. On my return I found that the relative had let my house to tenants. She filled her pockets with the rent money. The West Rand Administration Board, not getting its rent, raided my house, found strangers living there and took the house and sold it to another family.

'I kept getting news that my children were being moved from one welfare institution to another. The first thing I did when I got out of jail was to find my children. But I had no house. I approached the mayor of Soweto, David Thebehali and explained how I had lost my house. He promised to help me. But then another mayor took over, Ephraim Tshabalala, and then Edward Kunene. And with the mayors changing so often, I lost hope.

'I have little faith in talking to another mayor about my problems, as they don't seem to stay in office long enough to help one.'[1]

More often people are confronting 'false leaders.' Lindi Mahlatsi from Sebokeng in the Vaal area said, 'We want the mayor to resign. We are suffering because of him. If they can just meet our demands there won't be trouble in the township. They present themselves to the people as their savior. They said that they will lower the rent, but they are raising it.'

Gertrude Ngade said, 'They are undemocratic and useless. Only a handful of "ja-baas" [yes-boss] puppets.'

Talking to shop stewards

Virginia Matobela, 'Last week I was with my uncle who is the chairman of the Moca committee in Randfontein location - Mohlakeng. It's a bit like the old Soweto Committee of Ten, and is fighting against rent increases and for the pensioners. It is totally against the community councils.

'You know, with township problems — day to day ones — the people still talk of Sofasonke as the only honest man who ever really faced the government with the problems of Soweto. He used to call meetings with all the people before he took anything up with the government. These days the councillors keep secrets. They never really come to the people or consult. They run the townships on their own.

'Even if there are no people in the township which everybody respects, there is one person — Mandela. People are dying for him. Even the birds are dying for him. He knows the struggle and how people suffer. So everybody wants him. The way he got his education, and his history proves he knows the struggle. Not like Tshabalala who's really stupid and rich.'

Gladys Ndlovu said, 'And the councillors themselves, they always manage to choose the richest people as mayors — people who have never suffered.'

Elizabeth Kumalo, 'The councillors decide for us — but they

Women and Politics

are supposed to be for the people. Thebehali ran overseas to borrow money without consulting and now we must pay for it. We can't do that. And that's where the violence starts. But if you asked everybody if they would support Mandela it would be a big YES - with two raised hands.'

And about pensioners...Elizabeth Nelani, 'The councillors never talk of pensioners and other people in need. The pensioners have to stand in long queues even in the winter. They must queue sometimes from 4 o'clock in the morning. Unlike whites who can get their pensions any time from the post office.

'You see, people like Tshabalala they are willing to use the people against each other. If he does a favour and secures you a house, it is often through a bribe, and that means that a pensioner has probably been moved out of their house.'

But are there any solutions? Virginia Matobela said, 'In Soweto ... well you never know with these children, because they actually want no-one as a leader now. When you ask who could be good to be a councillor they say no-one, because all those councillors are keen on money.

'With the UDF — it's hard to meet them, or know of their events. I once met a guy who said he would call me if they have meetings, but they never tell us.'

Gladys Ndlovu said, 'Yes the UDF doesn't advertise things. But we also don't know of those civic associations. People are now scared of Azapo — they think they will end in jail with it.'

A meeting of community members at Crossroads.

And Virginia Matobela said, "Inkatha is strong because the people in it fight to keep it that way. The other day I was on the bus and heard some people talking about the stayaway, and Chief Gatsha's involvement at Secunda where over 6000 Sasol workers were fired for taking part in the November 1984 stay away. They were saying, how can he come to try and solve other peoples' problems while in Natal there is constant fighting between people. How can you sweep next door before you've swept in your own house? Gatsha is just a propaganda, a puppet.

Elizabeth Nelani, 'When you talk to the general people, sometimes they feel that they are scared to face politics in the open. Sometimes they want discussions privately. But not the children. They might already be spoiled because of the lack of education. But what little they have they'll use to fight — fight back for the whole history — for the days after the war when the British couldn't pay the Afrikaners who fought in the war, and so they paid with Africa — the children are not scared of death. They are just bold. They call us older people cowards.'

Rents

A woman said, 'Our problem is rents. Some earn about R40-R45 per week and others are unemployed. Take in consideration also the GST. The councillors force you to have lodgers if you can't afford rent. With some families they try to force them out of their homes. These problems extend into the married life of couples and destroy families.

'For long we have said that we have problems. But they don't listen. They just make the people frustrated.

'What is happening now is that anger has grown in our townships. When people were marching peacefully they were met with bullets of trigger happy boys. Later most people were shot along the way from work and some at bus-stops.

'It is worse when people went into jail only because they attended a funeral of Joseph Sithole. What do they expect us to do with our dead people? Must we eat the corpses?'[2]

FOOTNOTES:
(1) Sowetan Sunday Mirror, 20 January 1985.
(2) Speak Vol 2 No 4, November 1984.

Albertina Sisulu

Strydom You Have Struck A Rock

On August 9th 1956, 20 000 women went to Pretoria. The women were protesting against the extension of passes to African women. Albertina Sisulu was one of the 20 000.

To millions of South Africans, Albertina Sisulu needs no introduction. This 65 year-old grandmother represents for many, the suffering and the strengths of the South African people.

Albertina Sisulu came to Johannesburg to study nursing in 1942. She came from a poor family in the Transkei. In Johannesburg she met and married Walter Sisulu, one of the leaders of the African National Congress. He is now serving a life sentence in Pollsmoor Prison in the Western Cape.

Albertina Sisulu became involved in politics during the mass struggles of the 1950s. She was also involved in the Federation of South African Women which was formed in 1954.

Albertina Sisulu.

In 1964 Albertina was banned. For 17 years she lived under banning orders. During that time two of her children went into exile.

After her banning order was lifted in 1981, Albertina was once more thrown into the thick of opposition politics. She became actively involved in women's organisation in the Transvaal. When the United Democratic Front was formed in 1983 she was elected the Transvaal President.

'The Federation was formed on the 17th April 1954. The object of forming it was because women felt that it was high time they took their role as the mothers. In fact it was formed specifically to guard against injustices in their homes, families and their children.

'So the women decided to call all the women of all races to come together and discuss this and form a special organisation that would cater for their needs and objectives. To start with we called a few women from each group — the ANC Women's League, the Coloured People's Congress, the Indian Congress and the Congress of Democrats. It also included all the women in the trade unions — Sactu and so on.

'So we had a caucus and came to one conclusion — that we meet other women and form this organisation. So we called a conference that was held in Johannesburg at the Drill Hall. Every woman was there and we elected our office bearers. Our first president was Ida Mntwana who was also our president in the ANC Womens' League. In Cape Town we had Sonya Bunting, in Durban it was Florence Mkhize and in Port Elizabeth it was Florence Matomela.

'We went back to our areas to organise the women to join. We organised women from churches, sports, teachers — every woman was involved. It wasn't difficult to organise women, because the most affected women were African women.

'Also during that time there was the introduction of Bantu Education to our children, high rents were affecting us terribly and most of all we were affected by the introduction of passes for women. So these were the issues we organised women around. Everybody was interested in these issues, so many joined.

'Early in 1956 we called a conference to decide on a day of action and what the action would be to protest against passes. August 9th was decided and we decided to sign forms in protest to take to the Prime Minister — it was Strydom then. We would take forms straight to him.

'Every woman had a bundle of forms to be signed and we used that to organise the woman around passes and for the march. On the day we started early in the morning getting to the buses, to the trains, to the taxis, to whatever transport we could get to go to the Union Buildings.

'When we were assembling near the station a call came from the police that our march was banned. But we decided that our appointment with Strydom was not cancelled. We decided to go in twos, ones, until we got to the Union Buildings.

'We filled the amphitheatre of the Union Buildings and we elected a member from each group. From our group Lilian Ngoyi who was our second president from 1955, Helen Joseph from COD, Amina Cachalia from the Indian Congress and Sophie Williams from the coloured people.

' They took the forms to Strydom's offices. When they got to the office it was locked — the prime minister had run away. So they left the forms at the door. They came back to us and gave us the report. After that we sang Nkosi Sikelele, the national anthem.

'After that the Fed took off — every area knew there was an organisation for women. In those days there weren't problems organising women.

'The women came together and decided to close the schools because they felt that Bantu Education is inferior and poisonous to their children. So we closed the schools.

'The trouble started when men didn't take an active part in helping us. They were drinking in the beerhalls. We were annoyed and so we decided to close the beerhalls so that men should be interested in these important things.

'We organised cultural clubs and private schools, even in my house — we had a classroom here, we had teachers. But the government refused to register our schools so we couldn't continue. Funds were the big problem. So we let the children go back to school.

'After the 1950s there was a lull. The government was so repressive and there were bannings, detentions and banishments. To compare our organisation in the 1950s and organisation today — well in those days our organisations were open — they were not banned and there was discipline. Everybody was not just doing what she or he liked. This discipline led the people.

'The government used to listen to some of the complaints and perhaps relax the law. There wasn't so much torture, banning, harassment and detention of the people.

'Since then the government tactics have become too much for the people. Low salaries, with children to look after — well if the breadwinner is arrested, nobody is there to look after the home, and the children are starving. If the head of the family is sent to jail it makes the people afraid.

'Today — although the people are struggling, there is too much pressure from the government. Too many people are being killed.

'In the 1950s the police were seen more as men of the law. Today to see a policeman is to see a gun pointing at you.

'We are working for action, but also unity. So that if there is an issue we all think is important, women from all points of view will come together.

'The most important issues for women to organise around and educate themselves about today are mass removals, passes, influx control, the cost of living. The people experiencing mass removals suffer the most and the children suffer the most.

'These children are taken from a six-roomed house and dumped in a single corrugated iron room. Children of 15 years cannot sleep in the same room with their parents. And the children are dying. Look at Thornhill where the children died like flies.

'With general sales tax and rents we must work hard to educate women because not everybody knows what it means. Cost of living is something women must take up — not just accept. Women have to see to the food in the house and to the roof over our heads. Particularly the women from rural areas — they must be educated — they see the white man as a boss.

'In the 1950s we didn't really know that women could hold high positions as presidents of organisations. Men today I think accept women as equals. They have accepted the challenge. In the home too — if you go to a meeting you just instruct him that there is the food and you will find him having cooked for the children. They cook and clean and change napkins and sometimes even wash the napkins.'

The Women's

The Women's Charter was drawn up and adopted at the inaugural conference of the Federation of South African Women (FSAW), on 17 April 1954.

FSAW drew its members from the ranks of the four organisations which made up the Congress Alliance of the 1950s. They were the African National Congress, the South African Indian Congress, the South African Coloured Peoples Congress and the Congress of Democrats.

FSAW was the first women's organisation in South Africa to take a leading role in the political area. Its primary focus during these turbulent years was the campaign around the issuing of passes to African women.

Johannesburg — 17 April 1954

PREAMBLE: We the women of South Africa, wives and mothers, working women and housewives, Africans, Indians, European and coloured, hereby declare our aim of striving for the removal of all laws, regulations, conventions and custom that discriminate against us as women, and that deprive us in any way of our inherent right to the advantages, responsibilities and opportunities that society offers to any one section of the population.

A SINGLE SOCIETY: We women do not form a society separate from men. There is only one society and it is made up of both women and men. As women we share the problems and anxieties of our men, and join hands with them to remove social evils and obstacles to progress.

TEST OF CIVILISATION: The level of civilisation which any society has reached can be measured by the degree of freedom that its members enjoy. The status of women is a test of civilisation. Measured by that standard South Africa must be considered low in the scale of civilised nations.

WOMEN'S LOT: We women share with our menfolk the cares and anxieties imposed by poverty and its evils. As wives and mothers, it falls upon us to make small wages stretch a long way. It is we who feel the cries of our children when they are hungry and sick. It is our lot to keep and care for the homes that are too small, broken and dirty to be kept clean. We know the burden of looking after children and land when our husbands are away in the mines, on the farms, in the towns earning our daily bread.

We know what it is to keep family life going in pondokkies [small huts] and shanties, or in overcrowded one-room apartments. We know the bitterness of the children taken to lawless ways, of daughters becoming unmarried mothers whilst still at school, of boys and girls growing up without education, training, or jobs at a living wage.

Charter

POOR AND RICH: These are evils that need not exist. They exist because the society in which we live is divided into poor and rich, into non-European and European. They exist because there are privileges for the few, discrimination and harsh treatment for the many. We women have stood and will stand shoulder to shoulder, with our menfolk in the common struggle against poverty, race and class discrimination, and the evils of the colour bar.

NATIONAL LIBERATION: As members of the National Liberatory Movements and Trade Unions, in and through our various organisations, we march forward with our men in the struggle for liberation and defence of the working people. We pledge ourselves, to keep high the banner of equality, fraternity and liberty. As women there rests upon us also the burden of removing from our society all the social differences developed in past times between men and women which have the effect of keeping our sex in a position of inferiority and surbordination.

EQUALITY FOR WOMEN: We resolve to struggle for the removal of laws and customs that deny African women the right to own, or inherit property. We resolve to work for change in the laws of marriage such as are found amongst our African, Malay and Indian people, which have the effect of placing wives in the position of legal subjection to, and giving husbands the power to dispose of wives' property and earnings, and to dictate to them all matters affecting them and their children.

We recognise that the women are treated as minors by these marriage and property laws because of ancient and revered traditions and customs. Customs which had their origins in the antiquity of the people no doubt served purpose of great of value in bygone times.

There was a time in African society when every woman reaching marriageable age was assured of a husband, home and security. Then husbands and wives with their children belonged to families and clans that supplied most of their own material needs and were largely self-sufficient. Men and women were partners in a compact and closely-integrated family unit.

WOMEN AND LABOUR: Those conditions have gone now. The tribal and kinship society to which they belonged has been destroyed as a result of the loss of tribal lands, migration of men away from their tribal home, the growth of towns and industries and the rise of a great body of wage-earners on the farms and in the urban areas, who depend wholly on wages for their livelihood.

Thousands of African women, like Indian, coloured and European women, are employed today in factories, homes, offices, shops, on farms and in professions as nurses, teachers and the like. As unmarried women, widows or divorcees, they have to fend for themselves, often without the assistance of a male relative. Many of them are responsible not only for their own livelihood but also that of their children.

Large numbers of women today are in fact the sole breadwinners and heads of their families.

FOREVER MINORS: Nevertheless, the laws and practices derived from an earlier, different state of society are still applied to women. They are responsible for their own person and their children. Yet the law seeks to enforce upon them the status of a minor.

Not only are African, coloured and Indian women denied political rights, but they are also in many parts of the Union of South Africa denied the same status as men in such matters as the right to enter into contracts, to own and dispose property, and to exercise guardianship over their children.

OBSTACLE TO PROGRESS: The law has lagged behind the development of society, it no longer corresponds to the actual social and economic position of women. The law has become an obstacle to the progress of women, and therefore a brake on the whole society.

This intolerable condition would not be allowed to continue were it not for the refusal of a large section of our menfolk to concede to us women the rights and privileges which they demand for themselves.

We shall teach men they cannot hope to liberate themselves from the evils of discrimination and prejudice as long as they fail to extend to women complete and unqualified equality in law and in practice.

NEED FOR EDUCATION: We all recognise that large numbers of our womenfolk continue to be bound by traditional practices and conventions, and fail to realise that these have become obsolete and a brake on progress. It is our duty and privilege to enlist all women in our struggle for emancipation and to bring to them all realisation of the intimate relationship that exists between their status of inferiority as women and the inferior status which their people are subjected by discriminatory laws and colour prejudices.

It is our intention to carry out a nation-wide programme of education that will bring home to the men and women of all national groups the realisation that freedom cannot be won for any one section of the people as a whole as long as women are kept in bondage.

AN APPEAL: We appeal to all organisations, to members of the great National Liberatory Movements, to the trade unions and working class organisations, to the churches, educational and welfare organisations, to all progressive men and women who have the interests of the people at heart, to join us in this great endeavour.

Drawing Women Into The Struggle

The United Women's Organisation (UWO), is a mass-based organisation of women in the Western Cape. Members of the UWO executive were interviewed.

'The idea of forming the UWO was started in 1979 by eight women in Guguletu. We had all been involved in the Women's Federation in the fifties and sixties and so we knew that a women's organisation could help to mobilise the people.'

Setting up the United Women's Organisation

'1976 showed that parents were not able to support their children, and that there was something wrong in our society. We had fought Bantu Education when it was started in 1954, yet many parents became their children's enemy when they stood up against that education in 1976.

'We saw that we had no voice to speak for us or for our children. We knew that as women we were oppressed both in our houses and at work, and that we needed to work towards changing things as women, with both short and long term goals. So we worked towards the formation of a broad women's organisation in the Western Cape.

'There were residents' associations in Guguletu [township near Cape Town] with women's sections. But they were working within the framework of the government. When the rent issue came up in 1980, the people were not able to come together under the residents association. So we got together our core of women to work on the issue. We called mass meetings in the community. They have still not managed to increase the rents in Guguletu!

'UWO was set up as a non-racial organisation and that has been a major point all along. We organise around the problems women face in their day to day lives. But because people are forced to live in Group Areas [racially divided living areas] they don't all face the same problems. So we also choose uniting themes which are relevant across the lines of apartheid. These lines are forced on us. Building non-racialism is not an easy task. But for UWO it is a priority because we believe that South Africa belongs to all who live in it.

'We have always been clear that grassroots work and political work must go hand in hand. For example, at the same time we organise childrens' play groups we'll be working on an August 9th rally.

'We set up branches in different areas. Five people could form a UWO womens' group and when they had ten members a branch could be formed. Each branch had to look at the situation in that area and decide what to do there. We would come together once a month to assess our work, to support each other, and to give direction to the organisation as a whole.

'The exciting thing was that this intervention led to the formation of civics in some areas. In Guguletu in 1980 there were the school boycotts. A Parents Action Committee was set up. When the unrest ended people who had been active in UWO and in the Parents Action Committee came together to form a civic. We realised that we needed ongoing organisation, instead of just setting up a committee whenever there was a crisis.

'It wasn't as easy in other areas. Sometimes when a civic is already in existence we've been told, "We don't need a women's organisation here, our women are involved in the civic". Many women have been doing work in the civic, but they have never become leadership people.

'Eventually even the civics have realised that women's organisations are important. They help to train women, to give

Ma Zihlangu of the UWO.

them leadership and organisational skills. And this means that the women can participate more fully in the civics too. In some areas where the people have wanted to start a civic, UWO women have assisted in starting the civic. It is not a question of competition. Our aim is to draw women into the struggle. It does not matter if they stay in UWO or if they move into other organisations.

'But even now we find that in other organisations women are not given the chance to develop. We're trying to explore how we can support women in other organisations.

'Although UWO and progressive organisations each have their own programmes, we see one of our major roles as participating in united action with other progressive organisations.

'For example with the boycott of Fattis and Monis foods in 1979, the union asked us for support. So we participated in the planning of the campaign, calling public meetings, and we actively supported the workers. Our members would go to the place where they met everyday, to make them see that they had the support of the community.

'At our first conference, people who had been evicted from the Langa barracks single quarters in Langa township near Cape Town came to speak to us. They asked us to support them. They moved from a church in Langa to squat in the bush next to Nyanga another Cape Town township.

'In supporting the people of "Nyanga bush" we often acted as residents, to talk for them. We never used to take the organisation away from them, but worked as part of them, because many of them were new and scared.

'It's true that the borders between UWO work and the work of other groups is sometimes blurred. It has to be worked out in an ongoing way. But things change depending what each organisation is doing at a particular time. And our members always remain responsible to the organisation.

'One of the things that keeps UWO together is its structure. We have a tight structure with well organised committees and sub-committees. There is also a firm devotion to democratic functioning. This means that we can use the structure for very effective decision making and mobilisation.

'Our relationship to the United Democratic Front(UDF) is a good example. UWO was a very significant force in the formation of the UDF in the Cape. We helped to organise the conferences where UDF was discussed and finally launched, and our branches were in the forefront of creating UDF area committees. The idea for the signature campaign was debated through our structures and then raised in the UDF. So having the experience of how to structure and run the UWO, we have had a lot to contribute to the UDF.'

Organising themes

'It is important to say that as a women's organisation, we have a commitment to fight side by side with our men. We don't exclude men from our discussions, but they can't vote. At our conference men cook for us and run our creches.

'When it started, the UWO was the most high profile political organisation in Cape Town. So the men would come to us and ask what they could do. Our history has been a big factor in causing a strong relationship between us and other organisations. It has given women's organisation a legitimacy.

'In 1982 we chose two themes for the year — "Childcare" and "High Prices". On child care, each branch investigated ways of taking up the issue. We started play groups, and organised around International Children's Day and the United Nations Declaration of Children's Rights.

'Even with play groups, politics is important. One branch worked with the parent's committee of the play group in the hope that they would take up wider issues, and they did. They took up the removal of the "coloured" people from the area. They put out a booklet on the removals which people are still buying today.

'We held a mass meeting around the issue of high prices and especially the rise in the cost of bread. There was a resolution not to buy bread for a week. We got the shop owners to come and asked them, "Are you far away from us or are you with us?" And since then the shop owners have started moving with us. We also had plays and a procession.

'The themes for 1983 were "Childcare", the "Koornhof Bills" and the "Constitution". Our work within the UDF was also one of the main features for the year.

'At the end of January in 1984 we held a workshop to plan our direction for the year. We agreed to concentrate on drawing working women and church women into UWO. We have also been involved in ironing out our differences with the Women's Front, another women's organisation in Cape Town. Also the threat of removal to Khayelitsha is being taken up in the UDF area committees. The organisations involved in this campaign are the UWO, Cape Youth Congress (CAYCO) and the Civic (Western Cape Civic Association), because the issue affects everyone and we must fight it together.

'For National Women's Day in 1984, we worked with the UDF area committees to picket and hand out pamphlets. We held a joint UDF/UWO rally as the women's protest against the elections for the tri-cameral parliament.

'1984 was a difficult year for the women of South Africa. Things look to be worse in 1985. The high prices, the rents and

United Women's Organisation

> the unemployment will make our lives harder. But we in UWO know that these are the times when women stand up. Our branch in New Crossroads has stood with the women in their march to refuse to pay the rent increase. The spirit of these 200 women gives us the light for 1985.'

Bee Berman

A play performed by UWO members on 9 August 1984.

Our Yardstick Is Democracy

The Vaal Women's Organisation was formed in 1983. By September 1984, it was one of the largest and most organised women's groups in the Transvaal.

The organisation worked closely with civic and student organisations and trade unions in the Vaal area. The people in the Vaal found themselves faced with steadily increasing rents and service charges, and with a town council which was totally unsympathetic to their pleas.

After repeated appeals for no rent increases, the civic association announced that 3 September 1984 would be a work stay-away in protest against the increases. This was the day on which the increased rents were to come into effect.

Crowds gathered to make their opposition to the increases known. Police presence intensified. Eventually Sebokeng, the largest Vaal township, exploded into violence.

For months afterwards there was a constant police and army presence in the townships. Thousands of people were arrested and detained. Many more were injured with rubber bullets, birdshot and teargas.

During these months many activists were detained, arrested, or they simply disappeared.

Vaal Women's Organisation

The Vaal Women's Organisation was one of the casualties of this rebellion. Its leadership has been scattered. Some are in detention, others have disappeared, and many of its members have been intimidated to the point where they will not participate openly in its activities. By January 1985 women in the Vaal were regrouping and setting up a new women's organisation.

What follows is the group's description of the organisation early in 1984.

'A few women came together because they had problems which they felt were not being attended to. Those which were attended to were being given little attention. The other reason was, why do we have problems? For example, our children have no one to care for them while we're at work. The reason? The creches are full. Our children, especially teenage ones, are becoming delinquent. Why? Because they are not being taught the proper way.

'Why are our children without places — day care centres?

Vaal women's meeting in March 1894.

Vaal Women's Organisation

Now that they are full, why are more centres not built? If our children are delinquent because they are not properly taught, why are they not properly taught? Because parents are mainly concerned with work and when they come home have little to do with the children. Why are they not at school? Financial problems are restrictions, and many other reasons which point to black people being discriminated against and not fully catered for, if at all. There were no organisations that looked into the root of these problems.

'We women decided to do something about these problems. Firstly doing it practically eg. child minding, learning to sew, sewing to help ourselves financially. School uniforms are expensive so we set ourselves a task to sew school uniforms and knit jerseys at a cheaper price.

'That was not the end. Since we are discriminated against, we must speak out if we have a problem. If we do not speak out those who are in power will always say that we are satisfied. We must make those in power aware of what we want and what we do not want. We want nobody to decide for us without consulting us. We have to liberate ourselves. If we do not speak out we are firstly oppressing ourselves, which leads us to resort to deviant behaviour and in turn we are oppressed by those in power.

'The best idea was to form an organisation of women, an organisation that will represent the small groupings. With this there will be sharing of ideas, especially because the root cause of all our problems is the system of government.

'It is the mother who experiences problems first as she is the one caring for the family.

'To solve these problems, a group of eleven women came together during weekends. Eventually eight women ended up planning for a mass meeting where all women could come together to decide on the formation of this organisation.

' Pamphlets were written and printed. The meeting was also advertised in the newspapers and by word of mouth. We had planned to have the meeting announced in churches especially, but time was not on our side. We had been slow and the date already set. Rumour had it that the "system" [security police] would disrupt our meeting. So we distributed our pamphlets in the last two days. The odds were against us because there were undesirable elements who distributed false pamphlets on the last day, to tell people that the meeting had been cancelled.

'Our pamphlet called on people to come and discuss the most disheartening problems. Our pamphlet also listed names of prominent people to address us so that the people would know what sort of organisation to look forward to. Although we never succeeded, we should have had at least a small number of people representing each area as the Vaal is a big place. The Vaal Civic Association and the youth were called upon to assist.

'We are not thinking about ourselves only. We are not selfish about having a better life. All of us as black people are oppressed. We are concerned about the entire nation and its sufferings.

'There are other women's organisations like burial societies. But death is a small problem. We all have to die and be buried. The problem is in life, day after day we have problems. Unfortunately most organisations concentrate on death, maybe because it is an easier task to plan for burial. These organisations shun the task of challenging day to day issues. That is why the Vaal Women's Organisation was necessary. We look forward to working for change, complete change, however difficult.

'We are not an oppressive organisation laying down rules. The rules will be decided when we face our problems. We love and understand each other and that is why we want to unite. We are not interested in personal benefit.

'We are not an organisation of professional people, but we are a people's organisation, the people doing those things for themselves which are not catered for. Any person who seeks to fight oppression is welcome. We want to be assertive and fight for our rights. We recognise oppression of women by the law, our men, and discrimination by society and set out to fight against it. Our yardstick is democracy.

'The Vaal Women's Organisation is related to the Vaal Civic Association. Our problems are problems facing all people of South Africa, but some do not affect men directly.

'Some injustices are perpetrated on women only eg. sex discrimination. It is the woman who encounters most problems affecting the home. The question of doing some things for ourselves like undertaking projects eg. childminding, is facing women and has to be done by women.

'The civic association cannot reach everybody, especially women. But women's organisations will be able to do this, since there is the necessity to organise at all levels.

'The issues we hope to take up are:
- Challenging food and commodity prices with a bulk buying scheme.
- The issue of day care centres and child minding projects.
- Exploitation of parents by shops selling uniforms and enforcement of particular uniforms by schools while our children are being chased away from school, or failed. We will set up as many projects as possible and organise the community to support this cause (sewing, knitting, etc.).
- Co-operate with civic associations on all matters of concern.
- Challenge the issue of children being made scholar patrollers.
- Taking up the issue of widows and unmarried mothers being victimised by being evicted.
- Sex discrimination in all its forms.
- Food sold to our children at school and the existing bad canteens
- Children made to clean school premises and townships.
- The question of squatters.
- All forms of oppression.

'But there are difficulties when organising women. It is difficult to get money for transport, pamphlets, telephones etc. Our plans are disrupted by bad elements. Pamphlets are countered with announcements that meetings have been cancelled. Posters are destroyed. Youth organisations are very effective and fast in distribution. With no youth activists, this cannot be done well.

'House meetings are very effective. Sometimes, at the beginning poor women would not like meetings held in their houses because of an inferiority complex.

'The core group has to play a supportive role especially on the question of absenteeism, by following up what members' problems are. Being absent once may lead to a total stay away. If the core group does not play this role all goes badly.

'Also, long discussions always bore people. Some form of action will definitely encourage people. If political issues are the focus, and not the issues affecting people, women will show less interest. If people are not given a chance to participate women are discouraged and eventually stay away.

'Often men are oppressive and they do not allow their wives to join the organisation. They are afraid that the wife will be assertive and may outclass his status. Some men are police informers and bar their wives from coming to the meetings. Where the wife is aware of the man informing she is afraid to go to meetings.

'Police harassment at meeting places and at homes is a problem. For example, a woman was active in organising, and her house was watched every Saturday and Sunday morning. They would park their car right opposite her house for a few hours. Then they would follow her until she was at the meeting place. On the day of a meeting people are intercepted and asked where they are going and why they are going there.

'Some people used to besmirch the organiser's character, and discourage us from associating with her. Anonymous threatening letters are often sent to active members. Ministers of religion are also intimidated not to allow meetings at their churches. Some churches take the struggle from the people and believe that God will provide.

'Women are threatened with detention and are made to fear for their children's lives if it happens.'

It started with rents

In December 1984 a woman from the Vaal area said, 'In the Vaal we are struggling. The whole location is full of police knocking on doors every night picking up people. And the whole thing started with rentals. On 3 September when the riots erupted we were asking for our rents to be remitted. The councillors would not listen to us. The parents and the children joined hands and hell broke loose.

'The problem is that people in the Vaal get low wages and can't afford a rent of R65 or R78. As mothers we can't afford the rent. When a child is hungry the mother is affected, and she can't afford to educate her children because the rent is high.

'So now employers are deducting rent from the people's wages. The hostel dwellers are in a very bad situation. All their properties are taken from them so they can't go back to the homelands, until they pay rent. We have not paid for three months. And we won't pay until the councillors listen to our demands.'

Taking A Full Bus

In 1983, mass protests in Lamontville in Natal were sparked by the murder of Harrison Dube, a popular councillor and activist. It was said that Moonlight Gasa, the head of the Lamontville community council was responsible.

Dube had consistently opposed the introduction of high rents and service charges in the old, dilapidated and overcrowded township. His murder was seen as an attack on the community as a whole.

After Dube's death people refused to accept the new rents. They also rejected the community council system and the Black Local Authorities Act.

Demonstrations by Lamontville residents were marked by extreme violence from the authorities. This was kept secret until it was finally exposed in Parliament after many affidavits were collected testifying to police brutality.

In 1984, Lamontville was again the centre of community anger. This time the issue centered around attempts to incorporate the area into KwaZulu. The residents rejected this on the grounds that they would lose their South African citizenship and Section (10) rights.

Chief Gatsha Buthelezi insisted that the Lamontville people

wanted incorporation. Inkatha supporters clashed with residents who supported the Joint Rent Action Committee (JORAC), a federation of residents associations in the area, and the United Democratic Front.

Here the women of Lamontville talk about organisation during these turbulent times.

'The woman's group in Lamontville was formed in November 1983. Nobody knew where to get help. There was fighting after Mr Dube had been killed. Many police came in with teargas. It went on day and night.

'Police camped up in the hills by the clinic the whole month until July. People could not be on the streets at night. The police would come into the houses kicking the doors down and hitting people with sjamboks. The police tried to make the girls love them. Then there was the rent increase and the bus boycott as well.

'We women spoke about the problems. Children with no place to stay, no food, no work. At first 15 women joined the group. Each paid 50c a month.'

Meetings

'Now we meet at the church every week. We elected a chairperson, vice-chairperson, treasurer, vice-treasurer, secretary and vice-secretary and two organisers.

'A lot of women are finding it difficult to make meetings at night, six o'clock, because they have to cook for children and husbands. Some men do not like their wives to come out.

'We are talking about changing our meetings to a Saturday and Sunday instead of a weekday so that more women would be free to come. But women have carried on joining — we have grown to 100.

'We are a branch of the Natal Organisation of Women. We hope that there will be branches all over Natal.'

Organising

'In March we went to see the superintendent of Lamontville, Mr Turner, of the Port Natal Administration Board. He was prepared to close doors on people who had no money to pay rent.

'We organised as women because we thought we would be

Omar Badsha

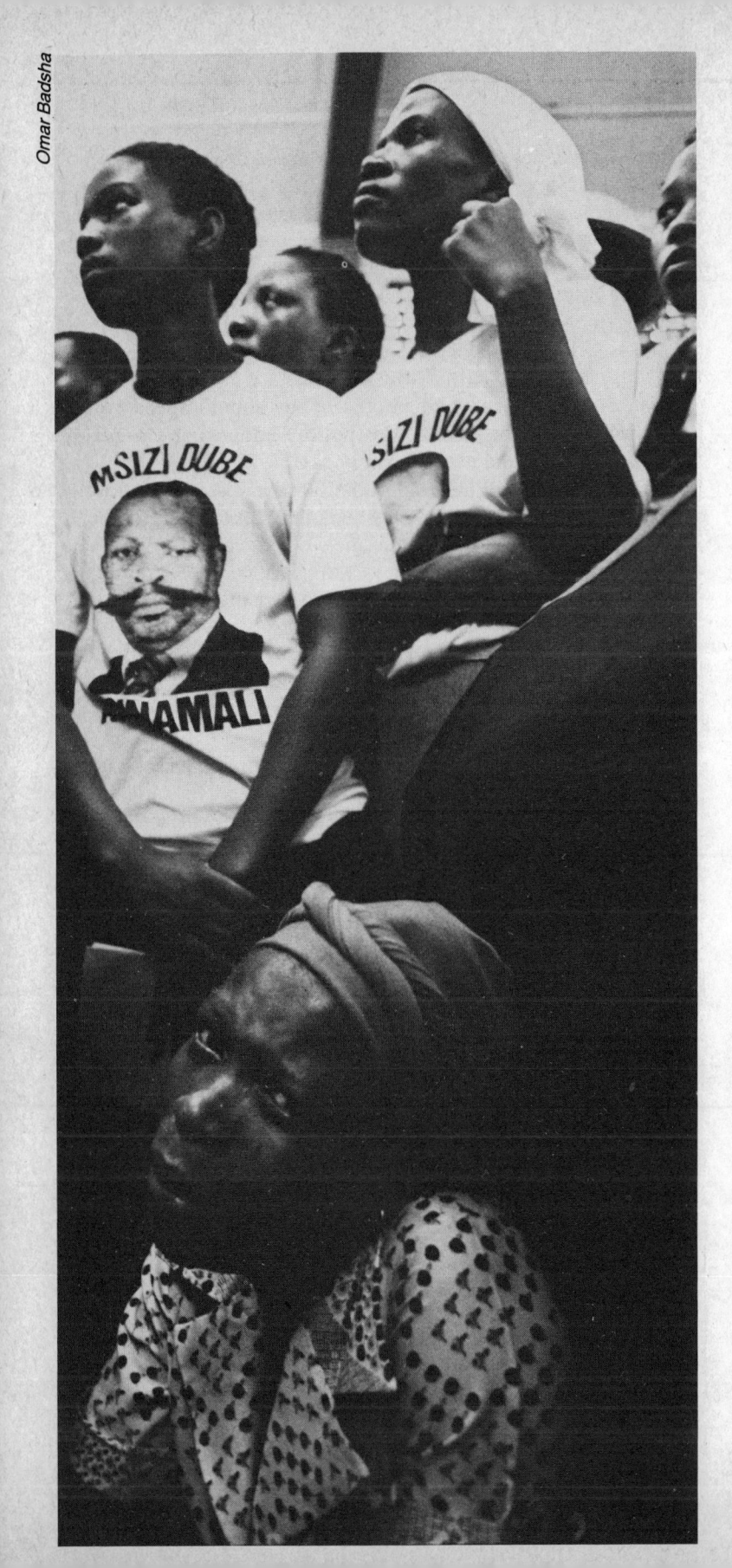

Msizi Dube's funeral at Lamontville.

safe from teargas and shooting. We could appeal on behalf of our children. We wrote a letter to take with us.

'When we came to Port Natal Administration Board the policeman at the gate said, "You're not allowed to see the Superintendent." We told him, "You're not allowed to stop us at the gate." So he let us in. At the Admin Board office we saw policemen gathering around with their guns. This did not worry us — nothing happened.

'We asked Mr Turner why the rents are going up when the houses are cracked and broken. They should speak to the people first and ask them why they are not paying rent before closing houses and taking furniture.

'Mr Turner said he would take our complaints to Mayville [suburb of Durban]. We knew he did not take our letter there. Instead, he took it to Mr Nxasane who is a councillor. He said we must talk to the councillors and not him. There is no point in going to the councillors. They do nothing for the people. Nothing has been done about the letter.

'We have asked Mr Turner where our reply is and he said, "They can't reply from Mayville, and I don't know why." When we said, "We want to go to Mayville." He said "You can't see them. You have to wait until I tell you."

'The rent and repairing of houses is becoming a real issue in Lamontville. Things were different before. The buses from Lamontville to town were 5c only and return was 10c. The rent for three-roomed houses was R1.25 per month. Four-roomed houses were R6 per month in New Look section. Flats cost R5 plus 20c for the school levy. There were no community councillors at that time.

'The houses were painted every year. When the windows were broken we would go to the office and they would be replaced. Now they just put plastic in. When the toilets jammed, the plumbers came and fixed them without charging. Now they don't come at all. They used to fix broken doors. If there were holes in the roof they would come and fix them.

'When the owner of the house was ill they would tell the office. The family would not have to pay until the owner was well again. When a person lost his job he was supposed to report until he got one. Now they just move people out and take the furniture away.

'And as we are women we say, "We must move forward, we cannot delay while things are so bad in Lamontville"'.

Other Activities

'The women's group does many other things. We want to do

Omar Badsha

sewing and knitting and crotchetting so that we can sell what we make for money. A lot of women cannot do it and others will teach them. We will use the money in the treasury to buy wool. Many of the women in the group are domestic workers and others are factory workers.

'We work with other organisations in Lamontville like Jorac, the Joint Commuters Committee (JCC) and Malayo, the youth organisation. There is a Joint Co-ordinating Committee where there are representatives of the Women's Group, Jorac, JCC and Malayo. If there is going to be a meeting or an issue in the community we all work together on it. We share costs too — say of a loudspeaker for a big meeting, each organisation must raise money for it.

'When there is a meeting we ask to speak for five minutes to tell the people about our Women's Group.

'We have discussions. For example we discussed that we do not want Lamontville to go to KwaZulu. The women said we must write a letter to the women of Hambanati and we have to ask the women of Chesterville and the women of Klaarwater [neighbouring townships], and all these women said we have to go and see Mr Koornhof about Lamontville's incorporation into KwaZulu. We will lose our Section 10 rights, and then belong to a homeland and have to pay R1 at the labour bureau to get a job — like Kwa-Mashu.

'We are thinking of taking a full bus to see Mr Koornhof — we will go as women and mothers. He can't shoot us.'

Dorothy Nyembe shortly after her release from prison, addressing the anniversary rally for FSAW, in Mamelodi.

Prison Cells

'Eleven Africans, including a woman, convicted of terrorism and communism, were sentenced to a total of 168 years imprisonment by Mr Justice Henning in the Supreme Court here today........The woman, Dorothy Nomzansi Nyembe, was sentenced to 15 years.'[1]

Little is known about the conditions of women political prisoners. Of what is known even less can be said, given the restrictions of the Prisons Act.

The Act states, 'Any person who publishes or causes to be published in any manner whatsoever any false information concerning the behavior or experience in prison of any prisoner or ex-prisoner or concerning the administration of any prison, knowing the same to be false, or without taking reasonable steps to verify such information (the onus of proving that reasonable steps were taken to verify such information being upon the accused), shall be guilty of an offence ...'[2]

It has been said that conditions in South African prisons leave much to be desired. Women political prisoners are only a small percentage of all political prisoners. Male prisoners often have others for company. Women political prisoners however, often serve their terms in almost complete isolation. In January 1984 there were 14 women political prisoners.

The following case of five women illustrates some of the conditions under which women political prisoners live.

In 1982, Caesarine Makhoere, Thandi Modise, Elizabeth Nhlapo, Kate Serokolo and Elizabeth Gumede, all serving sentences for terrorism, made application to the supreme court to improve their living conditions. They said that they were held in isolation, that they were denied any reading materials, and that the quantity and quality of their food was bad.

They described the conditions in their affidavits. 'Separate single cells, eight foot by eight foot, with space for a single bed, a small steel locker, a toilet and basin. Barred windows high up on the wall — you can look through by standing on the locker but this is not permitted.'[3]

Barbara Hogan, currently serving a ten-year sentence for treason in Diepkloof Prison, made an application for the alleviation of her conditions of imprisonment.

She said, 'For a considerable period of time since my admission to the Johannesburg Prison, I have been kept in isolation from other prisoners. I have also been confined to a separate wing of the prison away from any section in which other prisoners are accommodated. Since about 2 July 1983 I have again been totally segregated from other prisoners. It is not apparent to me why, in the circumstances, this has been deemed necessary. No allegation of breach of discipline has been made against me.'[4]

Bringing up kids in a prison cell...

'I am 28 years old and was arrested in 1981 and 1982 because I do not have a pass to live in Cape Town. I was convicted in the commissioner's court.

'The last time I went to prison my children were about four-years-old and two-years-old. Both times I was arrested my children accompanied me to gaol. Both children were ill with vomiting and diarrhoea. I was allowed to take them to the prison hospital but the nurse did not give them the right medicine.

'There were many of us in the cell ... about 30 or 40.

'There were no benches and we were each given a mat and two blankets for sleeping. We slept on the cold cement floor as there were no beds.

'During the day we cleaned our cell and the rest of the prison. The children stayed with us all the time. I would tie the baby on my back and the older one would just stand next to me.

'We never went outside for the whole five weeks.

'The warders confiscated the food I took with me to prison. I do not think friends were allowed to bring food or clothing. So we had no change of clothing, apart from one napkin for the baby which I had to give back when I left.

'We were woken at 5am and had a short time to wash ourselves and the babies. There was hot water. We fastened blankets with a safety-pin around us while we washed our clothes and waited for them to dry. We had to hang them on the windows of our cells or spread them over the mats on the floor to dry.

'In the mornings we had mielie meal, skim milk, a little bread and black coffee with no sugar.

'At lunchtime, we ate mielie rice, usually with a little meat. We had vegetables once a week and no fruit at all.

'In the evenings, we had porridge, mielie meal, coffee and a slice of dry bread, although sometimes it was spread with fat.

'I think the time in prison was hard for the children. The baby had bronchitis by the time I was released. We received far too little food and if we asked for more food it was refused. We also needed more blankets.'

The above interview appeared in a report published in December 1984 by the Institute of Criminology at the University of Cape Town.[5]

The Prisons Service replied[5], 'The prison authorities try at all times to ensure that children admitted to prisons are kept separately to avoid contact with hardened criminals....

'Policy provides that prisoners who are not engaged in programmes outside their cells are allowed periods of exercise of at least half an hour in the morning and half an hour during the afternoon outside their cells....

'Infants of women prisoners who are wholly or partially dependent on breast-feeding, and children who are fully dependent on their mothers are accommodated at State expense for as long as it is considered necessary. This also applies to babies who are born while their mothers are in prison. It is however policy to place small children in foster care as soon as possible....

'All prisoners, and infants or children are given a full physical examination by a physician soon after admission and as often as is necessary....

'Where accommodation permits, beds are provided, otherwise two mats and a minimum of three blankets are supplied.

'Dietary scales are revised continually by prison's service dieticians in co-operation with the Department of Health and Welfare....'

FOOTNOTES:
(1) The Star 26/3/69.
(2) Section 44 1(f) (i) Prisons Act.
(3) Applicants' founding affidavit in Case No 13122 of 1981.
(4) Applicant's founding affidavit in Case No 21275 of 1983.
(5) The interview and the Prison Service replies are drawn from newspaper reports. Bringing up kids in a prison cell, Rand Daily Mail, 21/12/84. What the Prisons Service says about this Report, The Star, 21/12/84.

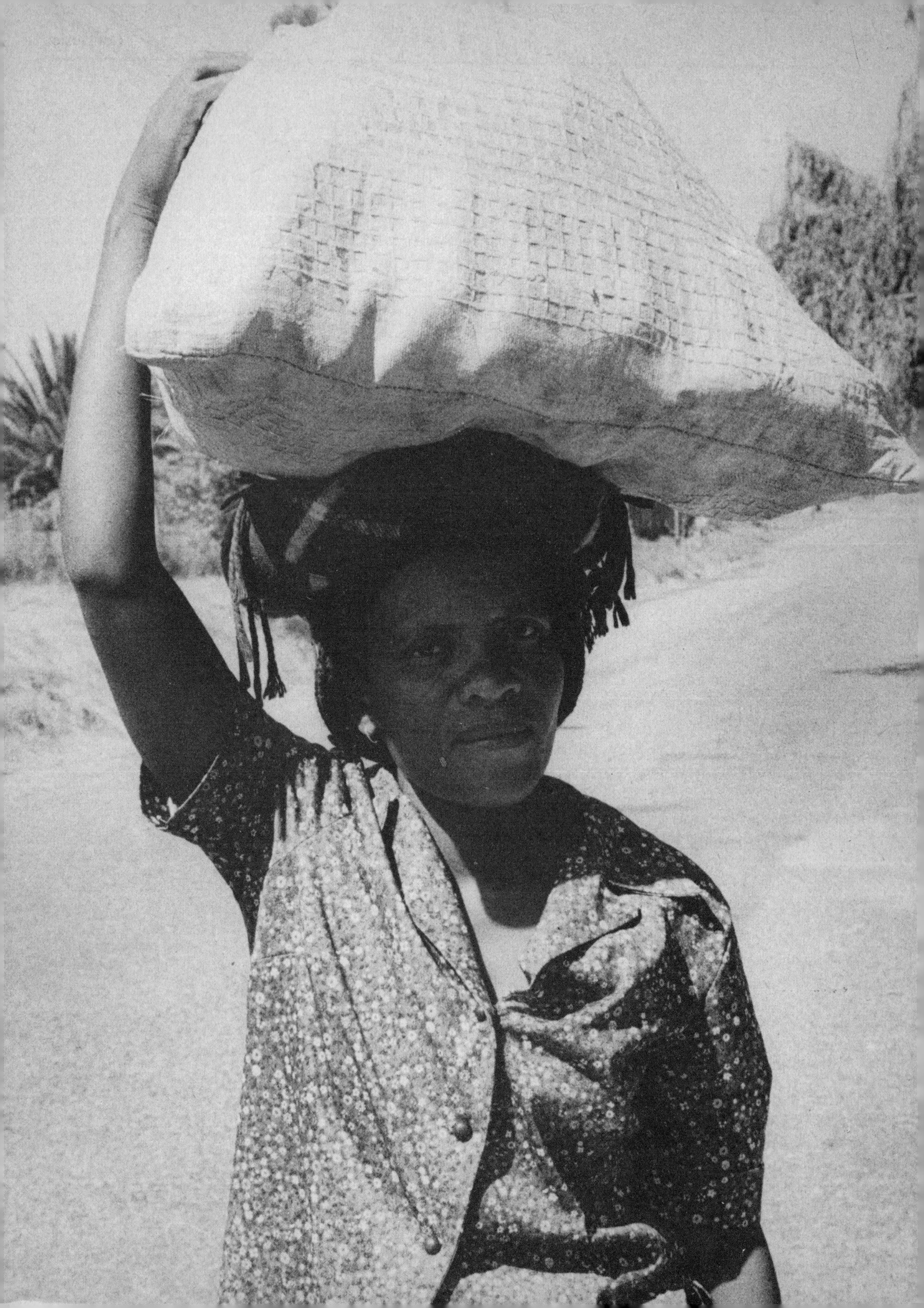

Until All Women Are Involved

Throughout the pages of this book, we have read the stories of many women. Stories of pain and suffering, stories of anguish; these are women whose lives are characterised by unending work, and unending stress. There is little taste of joy, and little taste of leisure.

But above all, the mood of these women is a mood of determination and endurance. Whether caught in a desperate struggle to feed their children, or washing office floors in the still hours of the night, women's daily experience speaks of a will to survive. Not only survival for themselves, but for their children.

The stories are endless.

● The experience of women in Cape Town, their houses bulldozed by police. Plastic sheets serving as shelters from the winter rain. Forced onto buses heading for the barren Transkei, they return undaunted within a few days, to reclaim their right to live with their husbands in a place where there is work.

● The experience of women in a factory. Forced to have sex with a supervisor in order to get a job. But they get together and make a plan to catch the supervisor as he tries to rape a new employee. And they get him fired.

● The experience of women on a factory farm working for

Conclusion

R47 a month. The women work for 14 hours a day. There is no other work to choose from, but they strike to demand better conditions and better pay.

These are three stories of will and determination against all odds.

African women's lives are lives of class exploitation and sexual and racial oppression. To organise effectively, women must understand how these factors work. In the present political situation people must also decide on priorities, the main issues to organise around. There is a bitter struggle for economic and political rights. But women's issues must have a place in this struggle. Only women can find the ways to do this.

In June 1984, the Transvaal Fedsaw Interim Co-ordinating Committee held a workshop to look at the roots of women's oppression. They discussed how to respond to these problems in women's groups, and in the broader political arena.

Women's important position in society was summed up,

Gill de Vlieg

'Women are the ones who bear all the pain, yet they are the pillars of strength in the family and the community.'

Women at the workshop talked about their oppression in ways which reflect the essence of this book. The points they made are a fitting conclusion to much of what we have already said.

Their first concerns were problems specific to women. 'Women have to face violence and rape. We also have to deal with "sexy" bosses at work. Menstruation and pregnancy also mean that there are special problems which we face as women.

'Because we are taught that we are inferior from childhood, women lack confidence in themselves. Our male comrades take us for granted and don't always show us respect. They also tell us what our women's groups should be doing. Because of all this, we are afraid to talk in meetings — so the men think we have nothing to say.'

'As women we have to look after the children and the house. This means that we have to deal with all the financial burdens, the rising prices, GST, increases in community services. We also have to see to the education of our children. So we are the ones who take all the responsibility — we are the sponges at the bottom absorbing all the shocks.'

Culture and tradition, women said, could be chains that bind people. 'Our traditions and culture make us believe that we are weak and inferior. Even our churches make us believe that we are weak. So our traditions and our culture discriminate against us.'

...and of course the issue of racism. 'As women we have to face all the problems of low wages, lack of confidence, caring for the family and so on. But it is African women who are really at the bottom of the pile, because they have to face pass laws, influx control and all the other apartheid laws in our country.'

Women's organisations are part of the liberation struggle. But often it is difficult to draw women into organisations.

'We need women's organisations because of the special problems that we face as women. In our separate women's groups we can talk about all these things. Because women are not taught to be in competition with each other, we can talk easily to each other. We can look at how women see themselves, why we think we are weak, and we can learn to have confidence in ourselves and our abilities.

'In our groups we can share our problems. A problem shared is a problem cut in half. When we come together to discuss our problems we also learn that talk is not just gossip but leads to action. In our groups we can educate ourselves about the struggle in our country. This we can use to teach our children.

'We as mothers, are the first teachers of our children. We are the ones teaching future generations. We can use our work with other organisations to make sure that we know all there is to know about our struggle and our situation. Without getting this knowledge for ourselves, we cannot hope to educate our children in a responsible way. Nor will we be able to teach other women.'

'We need a women's organisation so that we can teach our men that women are not babies, that they should respect us and understand that we also have a role to play in the struggle. This struggle will never be won until all the women are involved as well.'